Murder Most Vile
Volume Two
18 Truly Shocking
Murder Cases

Robert Keller

Please Leave Your Review of This Book At
http://bit.ly/kellerbooks

ISBN-13: 978-1535195454
ISBN-10: 1535195452

© 2016 by Robert Keller

robertkellerauthor.com

Table of Contents

Wife, Mother, Murderess

At around 10:50, on the night of Thursday, May 19, 1983, a late-model red Nissan Pulsar with Arizona plates pulled up to the ER at McKenzie-Willamette Hospital in Springfield, Oregon. The driver, a blonde woman in her twenties, staggered from the vehicle. "Somebody just shot my kids!" she screamed pointing back towards the car.

ER medics are of course used to dealing with such situations. Nurses Rose Martin and Shelby Day were out of the door in an instant, running towards the woman. Seeing that she was only slightly injured they pointed her inside, then went to the aid of her passengers. Meanwhile, receptionist Judy Patterson, as is protocol in such cases, got on the phone to the police.

The first thing that nurses Martin and Day saw as they approached the car was blood, lots of it, sprayed across the interior, spattering the bodies of three small children. A blonde-haired girl was slumped in the passenger seat, another girl and a boy, no more than a toddler, in back. All appeared to have suffered gunshot wounds to their chests.

The children were pulled from the vehicle and rushed into the hospital where it was determined that one of them, the girl who had been in the front seat, was already dead. Meanwhile, with personnel from the ICU brought in to assist, a battle was waged to save the other two. Thanks to the skill of the medical professionals involved, 8-year-old Christie Downs and her 3-year-old brother, Danny, would eventually pull through. The dead girl was their sister, Cheryl, aged just 7.

Police officers from both Springfield and Lane Counties had in the interim responded to the call and it was quickly determined that the crime fell within the jurisdiction of the Lane County Sheriff's Office. Sergeant Robin Rutherford then spoke to the children's mother. She said that her name was Diane Downs and that she'd been driving to her home in Springfield, after visiting a friend in Marcola. As she'd turned onto Old Mohawk Road, a man had flagged her down. He'd demanded her keys. When she refused to hand them over, he leaned into the car and fired at her children.

Without waiting to get the finer details, Rutherford immediately put out an APB on the suspect. If there was a madman on the highway, taking potshots at travelers, he needed to be apprehended before he could shoot anyone else. Diane Downs described the perpetrator as, "white, late-twenties, about five feet nine, 150 to 170 pounds, dark wavy hair, a stubble of beard, wearing a denim jacket and an off-colored T-shirt." Yet despite quick action by the police, despite an exhaustive search, no trace of the mystery gunman was found.

And it wasn't long before officers began to wonder whether he even existed. Something about Diane Downs' story, about her demeanor, just didn't sit right. She was too calm for one thing. Someone who had come through such a terrifying experience, losing one of her children, seeing others severely injured and not yet out of danger, would have been devastated, traumatized. Diane was calm and dry-eyed. On hearing that her middle child, Cheryl, had died, she registered no emotion. When she learned that Danny was going to make it, her response stunned medical staff. "You mean the bullet missed his heart?" she said incredulously. "Gee whiz!"

And the crime scene itself caused law officers to question her story. The stretch of highway between Marcola and Old Mohawk Roads was dark, desolate and eerie. Why, they wondered, would a young mother, with three small children in the car, stop for a total stranger in such an isolated spot?

Another cause for suspicion was the wound to Diane's arm. Those officers who'd been on the job more than a few years had seen that kind of injury before. Usually, it was self-inflicted by criminals who wanted to create the impression that they were the victim, rather than the perpetrator.

All of this was, of course, conjecture. Downs had said that she'd stopped because she thought the man needed help and that might be true. As for her demeanor, well, we all deal with grief and trauma in our own way. Better to focus on the physical evidence. Of that, there was plenty.

It was determined that the weapon used had been a .22, probably a handgun; powder burns on the children's skin suggested that the shots had been fired at extremely close range; blood spatters indicated that the shooter had fired from the driver's side of the vehicle.

This tied in with Diane Downs' story. She said that she'd been returning from visiting a co-worker, Heather Plourd. On the drive home, she'd decided that she'd take Old Mohawk Road rather than the highway because she thought it might be, "fun to go sightseeing." It was just after making the turn that she spotted the man, standing in the middle of the gravel road, signaling for her to stop.

She applied the brakes and got out of the car. The stranger approached, then produced a pistol from his jacket and demanded her car keys. She refused to hand them over, whereupon he leaned in through the driver's window and fired at her children. He then reached for her, but she evaded his grasp, got into the car and got the engine started. He fired one more shot, hitting her in the arm. Then she mashed her foot down on the gas and raced away. Her only thought, she said, was to get her kids to the hospital.

The next step in the investigation was to carry out a search of Diane's home. She willingly agreed, informing officers that she kept a .38 revolver and a .22 caliber rifle there for self-protection. Neither weapon had been fired recently but the police nonetheless took both into evidence, along with a diary.

Meanwhile, Diane's vehicle was transported to the crime lab for further investigation, and the body of Cheryl Downs went to the morgue for autopsy. Then Diane was allowed in to see her daughter Christie, who was now out of surgery and stable. Several nurses and a police officer were present at this visit. All would later testify to Christie's strange reaction to her mother's presence. As Diane approached the bed and whispered a faint, "I love you," Christie's eyes appeared to widen in fear, while the monitor measuring her heart rate jumped from 104 beats per minute to 147.

The day after the shootings, the case was assigned to rookie Assistant DA Fred Hugi. Despite his relative inexperience, Hugi took one look at the evidence and decided that something was amiss. And those inklings of doubt only increased after he interviewed Diane Downs. Her description of the harrowing event was nonchalant, even peppered with humor at times. Not only that, but she kept making subtle enhancements to her story, as though the added details would lend credibility.

Another reason to question Diane's version of events was a piece of information gleaned from the children's father, Steve Downs. According to Downs, his former wife had not been entirely honest about her weapons cache. She also owned a .22 pistol, he said. Asked about this, Diane flatly denied ever owning such a weapon.

Hugi didn't believe her and now made finding that weapon his number one priority. But an extensive search of the area surrounding the crime scene, even sending divers to the depths of the nearby Mohawk River, did not turn it up. And there was more bad news for Hugi when doctors informed him that Christie

Downs had suffered a stroke. The child was probably the only one who could testify as to what had really happened that night. Now doctors were saying that she might never recover fully enough to do so.

Despite these setbacks, ADA Hugi was more certain than ever that Diane Downs had been the shooter. One question, though, still bothered him. Why? Why would a young mother brutally gun down her three young children? In order to find the answer, he decided to look into Diane's background and dispatched investigators Doug Welch and Paul Alton to Arizona, where she'd lived until recently.

Diane had worked as a mail deliverer out of the Channing post office. Co-workers there didn't have anything particularly negative to say about her, but there were not many who had a kind word either. What emerged was a picture of a determined, yet insecure woman, a woman with a warped sense of priorities. She refused, for example, to deliver copies of Playboy magazine on her route, yet at the same time, it was common knowledge that she slept around. Steve Downs had told investigators that his former wife liked to "bed hop." In Arizona, investigators found plenty of evidence of that.

Diane's most recent beau had been one of her co-workers, Robert Knickerbocker. When the officers interviewed Knickerbocker, he said that he'd become involved with Diane shortly after her divorce from Steve Downs in 1981. She had actively pursued him and he, knowing her reputation, had gone along, thinking that the affair would amount to nothing more than a few sexual encounters with no strings attached. Instead, he'd landed himself in a "Fatal

Attraction," situation. Diane was soon pressing him to leave his wife for her. Knickerbocker then tried to break off the affair but Diane refused to let go.

Matters eventually came to a head when Diane insisted that he choose between her and his wife. Knickerbocker told her that he still loved his wife. After that, he confessed the affair and he and his wife were reconciled. But Dianne continued to stalk him, once even confronting his wife at their home and on another occasion pounding on their front door for hours and screaming obscenities.

That was in February 1983. Not long after, Diane put in for a transfer to Oregon and moved to Springfield to be close to her parents. But she continued harassing her old boyfriend with letters and phone calls.

Knickerbocker shared two other important pieces of information with the officers. He confirmed Steve Downs' assertion that Diane had indeed owned a .22 handgun. He also provided the officers with a possible motive for the shootings.

On one occasion during the relationship, Diane had showed up to meet him with her kids in tow. Knickerbocker had left immediately, saying he didn't want to spend time with her while she was with her kids. His reason for this, he explained to the officers, was because he didn't believe that the children should be exposed to their mother's infidelities. However, Diane had interpreted it differently. She became obsessed with the idea that Knickerbocker only wanted to end the relationship because of her

children. Armed with this information, the detectives returned to
Oregon.

In June 1983, Assistant DA Hugi called a meeting of his
investigative staff to determine if they had enough to arrest Diane
Downs for murder. The conclusion was that, despite strong
circumstantial evidence, the absence of the murder weapon meant
that they probably didn't. Nonetheless, a grand jury was
assembled to hear testimony in the case.

During the nine months that those proceedings lasted, Diane
Downs became something of a media darling, appearing in
tabloids and newspapers up and down the Pacific coast. Most
media depicted her as an innocent woman who been through a
terrible ordeal and was now having her grief compounded by
being dragged through the courts. Contributing to this image,
Diane got herself pregnant by a new lover and used this in the
press. She said that she'd decided to have another child because
she missed Christie and Cheryl and Danny so much. (Christie and
Danny had been placed in foster homes by a judge.)

In February 1984, the grand jury announced its ruling. They
indicted Downs on one charge of murder, two charges of
attempted murder, and two charges of criminal assault.

The matter came to trial at the Lane County Courthouse, in
Eugene, Oregon, on May 10, 1984. By then, it was a sensation
across America, with people divided as to whether Diane Downs
had gunned down her children or not.

There were several moments of high drama during the trial, most notably when the jury was transported to the crime scene, and when they were allowed to view Downs' blood-spattered Nissan Pulsar. The most dramatic interlude, though, was the testimony given by Christie Downs.

Shivering and teary-eyed, speaking in a barely audible voice, Christie was asked, "Who shot you?"

"My mom," she said simply.

After that, the case was lost to Diane Downs. Almost overnight, public opinion swung against her. She went from martyr to demon in the blink of an eye. When the jury announced its decision on June 14, 1984, no one was surprised that it was, "Guilty."

Diane Downs was sentenced to life in prison, with fifty years added for using a firearm in the crime. Not long after sentence was passed she gave birth to a daughter who she named Amy. The child was subsequently adopted.

In 1987, Downs pulled off a daring escape from the Oregon Women's Correctional Center. She remained at large for 10 days, before being captured less than a mile from the prison. As a result of that escapade, she was transferred to the maximum-security Clinton Correctional Institution in New Jersey. She remains there to this day.

Danny Downs was confined to a wheelchair as a result of his injuries, while Christie made a full recovery. Both were adopted by Fred Hugi, the Assistant District Attorney who had successfully prosecuted their mother.

The Ugly Death of a Beauty Queen

Sunday, February 2, 1986, was a warm day in Sydney, Australia. Twenty-six-year-old Anita Cobby, a registered nurse and former beauty queen, had worked a shift at the hospital, finishing at three that afternoon. She then agreed to have dinner with a couple of her nursing colleagues, phoning her father to tell him of the arrangement.

After dinner, one of Anita's friends drove her to the railway station. There, she boarded a train for the Sydney suburb of Blacktown, where she lived with her parents, Garry and Grace Lynch. Although married, Anita was separated from her husband, John. The two remained on good terms.

Anita had agreed to phone her father once she reached Blacktown station so that he could pick her up. However, the public telephone was out of order. She then walked to the taxi rank but there were no cabs available. The Lynch residence was a half-hour away. It was a pleasant evening. Anita decided to walk.

At the same time, a gang of local thugs was cruising the neighborhood in a stolen car. Their leader was John Travers, just 18 years old but already a habitual criminal with a rap sheet that included arrests for burglary, theft, larceny, drug abuse, rape, and bestiality. Also in the car were Michael Murdoch, a childhood friend of Travers, and the Murphy brothers, Michael, 33, Gary, 28, and Les, 24.

Anita was walking along Newton Road when the men spotted her. Gary Murphy was at the wheel and Travers immediately instructed him to pull up beside her. Then the other two Murphy brothers jumped out and dragged her, kicking and screaming, into the car. They sped off into the night, with Anita in the backseat.

Anita begged them to let her go. She told them that she was married and that she currently had her period. It was to no avail. The men told her to strip. When she refused, they started beating her, punching her over and over again, breaking her nose and her cheekbone, causing extensive bruising to her face, breasts and shoulders. They then ripped off her clothes and began raping her in the car, stopping only when they pulled in at a gas station to fill the car, using money they'd taken from Anita's purse.

After filling the vehicle, they drove to a field off Reen Road where Anita was pulled from the car and dragged through a barbed wire fence. There the assault continued. Anita was forced to perform oral sex on each of the men and was raped again. At times, two of the men were sexually assaulting her simultaneously.

Eventually, they tired of their bestial attack. Then a discussion took place as to what they should do with Anita. It was decided that, as she could identify them, they were going to have to kill her. John Travers volunteered to carry out the murder. He sat on Anita's back and pulled her head back by the hair. Then he placed his knife against her throat. Yet, even now, Anita fought for her life. She got a grip on the blade and tried to wrench it away, deeply lacerating three of her fingers in the process. It was to no avail. Travers inflicted three knife wounds, hacking so deep that he almost decapitated her.

The men then drove away from the scene, abandoning the car after setting it alight. Travers later burned Anita's clothes at his house.

Anita's parents were not too concerned when she didn't return home that night. She often slept over at a friend's house if she was out late and they presumed that's what had happened. However, the following afternoon, the Sister on Anita's ward called to enquire about her, as she hadn't shown up for work. Anita's father then began frantically phoning friends and family, trying to establish if anyone had seen her. When those calls proved fruitless, he went to Blacktown Police Station and reported his daughter missing.

The missing person report was filed at 7 p.m. on February 3, not quite 24 hours since Anita had last been seen alive. Early the following morning, police detectives Graham Rosetta and Hugh Dundas were called to a field in nearby Prospect, where a woman's body had been found. The brutalized body was naked, lying face down in a pool of congealed blood. It was evident that she'd suffered a vicious beating. Her throat had also been slit, the deep cuts running all the way to the spinal column. Although the woman matched the general description of Anita Cobby, it wasn't certain yet that this was her. The only identifying feature was the wedding ring she wore on her finger.

While the body was transported to the morgue at Westmead Hospital, the ring was taken into evidence. It was later shown to Anita's family, who said that it was similar to the one she wore. However, that did not suffice as positive identification. Someone had to view the body and that unenviable task fell to Anita's father, Garry. "Yes," he said, after looking for a moment at the broken body on the autopsy table. "That's my daughter."

By now the story was headline news in the Australian media, sparking an unprecedented outpouring of public anger. The police were inundated with calls from angry citizens calling for the swift apprehension of the perpetrators. Petitions were launched, gaining thousands of signatures, demanding the reinstatement of the death penalty. Radio talk shows and newspaper columns were deluged with messages, both supporting the grieving family and venting anger at the killers.

On February 6, the New South Wales State Government put up a $50,000 reward for information leading to the apprehension of the killers. On February 9, a week after Anita's murder, the police staged a re-enactment of Anita's last known movements. The event was filmed and televised in the hope that it might jolt someone's memory.

The re-enactment produced an instant result. A teenager named John McGaughey came forward to say that he and his sister had seen Anita being dragged into a white and gray Holden Commodore at around 9:50 p.m. on that Sunday evening. McGaughey had even run after the car in an attempt to help the woman, but the car had sped off. Later, he'd told his older brother, Paul, about the incident and Paul had gone driving, looking for the car. He'd spotted a similar vehicle parked along a desolate stretch of road but it was a different model to what his brother had described, so he drove on. In fact, it was the right car. At the time Paul spotted it, Anita was being raped in the bushes just a dozen yards away.

Anita Cobby's funeral took place on Monday, February 10, 1986. A week later, the police had their first break, when an informant mentioned the name John Travers in connection with the stolen vehicle that had been used in the abduction. Travers was, of course, well known to the authorities, and it was also common knowledge who his regular associates were. On February 21, Travers was eventually tracked down and arrested, along with Michael Murdoch and the Murphy brothers. All were charged with car theft, after which Murdoch and the Murphys were released on bail.

Travers, though, remained in custody. The police had questioned him about the murder of Anita Cobby and, although he denied any involvement, his answers were contradictory. The police were convinced that Travers knew more that he was telling. However, he stoically maintained his innocence. They were going to have to try something else to get him to talk. Then, Travers provided them with a way.

While in custody, Travers insisted that a female friend be allowed to visit him, so that she could bring him some cigarettes. The investigating officers immediately saw an opportunity. They acceded to the request but spoke to the woman before she went in to see Travers and convinced her to wear a wire. Although terrified of Travers, the woman agreed. When she later mentioned the murder to Travers he began boasting about it, implicating his four cohorts as well. Twenty-two days on from the brutal slaying, all five of the perpetrators were in custody.

The trial of John Travers and his co-accused began at the Supreme Court of New South Wales, in Sydney, on March 16, 1987. Travers pleaded guilty, while the other defendants spent the next 54 days accusing him, and each other, of the murder, while proclaiming themselves innocent. It did them no good.

On 10 June 1987, all five men were found guilty of murder. On June 16, all five were sentenced to life imprisonment, without the possibility of parole.

An Eye for An Eye

The state of Texas has more death row inmates and executes more prisoners than any other in the Union. But few of the executions it has carried out can have been as controversial as that of Karla Faye Tucker. For starters, Karla Faye was female, and the Lone Star state hadn't put a woman to death since the Civil War. Then there was the fact that Karla was under the influence of drugs when she committed murder and strong evidence that there was no premeditation. Either of these factors might have mitigated the sentence. Still, the double homicide perpetrated by the petite 24-year-old was one of the most brutal in the state's history. Many believed that Karla Faye fully deserved what she got.

Karla Faye Tucker was born in Houston, Texas on November 18, 1959, the youngest of three daughters. Her father, Larry, was a longshoreman in the Gulf of Mexico, her mother Carolyn, a homemaker.

On the surface, the Tuckers were a happy family. They often vacationed at a   cottage they owned on Caney Creek in Brazoria, Texas, and those days would later be remembered as the happiest of Karla Faye's life. But that happiness was an illusion. Karla's parents had a tempestuous relationship, marked by infidelity by both parties. They divorced and remarried several times. Karla would later discover that Larry was not her biological father, but that she'd been sired by one of her mother's many lovers.

By that time Larry and Carolyn had split for good. Karla Faye was ten years old when her parents finally dissolved their marriage and she and her sisters went to live with their father.

Larry had a difficult time controlling his three young daughters. At the time, he was working double shifts and was rarely home, leaving the girls to do pretty much as they pleased. By the age of 10, Karla Faye had already been introduced to marijuana by her sisters. By 11, she was shooting heroin. A year later, she and her sisters began hanging out with a local motorcycle gang called the Banditos. She lost her virginity to one of the bikers when she was just 12 years old.

Eventually, Larry Tucker threw in the towel with his uncontrollable daughters and shipped them off to their mother. Things got no better there. Carolyn was by then working as a prostitute and after Karla dropped out of school in the middle of the seventh grade, Carolyn encouraged her to take up the trade herself. By age 14, Karla Faye Tucker was working as a prostitute.

When Karla Faye was 16, she met and married a mechanic named Stephen Griffith. The marriage was tumultuous. Despite her tender years, Karla was already a hardened veteran of the sex and drugs scene and the couple fought constantly, leading to their eventual separation. Griffith would later recall their time together with affection. Karla Faye was tough and feisty, he said, qualities he appreciated in a woman. "We fist-fought a lot. I've never had men hit me as hard as she did. Whenever I went into a bar, I didn't have to worry because she had my back."

After leaving Griffith, Karla drifted to Houston's tough Quay Point neighborhood, where she continued working as a prostitute. She met and befriended Shawn Dean, and through her was introduced to 37-year-old Danny Garrett, a self-described "pill doctor." She and Garrett would become lovers. Both Garrett and Dean would be key players in the events to follow.

On Sunday, June 13, 1983, Karla was at a party in Houston, a birthday celebration for her sister, Kari Ann. The party had been going for three days and the steady flow of beer, whiskey and tequila, not to mention valium, mandrax, cocaine, LSD and other drugs, ensured that the festivities were still in full flow. Several times during the celebration, clothes were shed and the celebrants engaged in a sex orgy.

Much of the talk at the party had been about Shawn Dean's separation from her husband, Jerry Lynn Dean. Shawn had arrived sporting bruises and a broken nose, something that had incensed Karla. She and Jerry Lynn had a longstanding hate/hate relationship. Several times during the party Karla spoke about driving over to Jerry's apartment and beating him up. She was talked out of doing so. Nonetheless, she, Shawn, Danny Garrett and another friend, Jimmy Leibrandt, continued to rage about Jimmy's treatment of his wife.

At around mid-evening on that Sunday, Danny had to leave the party to go to his job as a bartender at a local tavern. Karla dropped him off at work, returning with Jimmy Leibrandt at 2 a.m. to pick him up. By then, Danny had had time to think about how to get revenge on Jerry Dean. Once in the car, he announced his plan. They were going to drive to Dean's apartment and steal his beloved Harley Davidson motorcycle.

Both Karla Faye and Jimmy loved the idea. What better way to get to Jerry Lynn than to jack his hog? There could be no greater insult to a biker. They decided to carry out their plan right away and instructed Jimmy to point his car in the direction of Jerry Lynn Dean's apartment.

Dean's ground floor apartment stood aside a vacant lot on a dimly lit street. As they approached, Leibrandt turned off the car's headlights and allowed the vehicle to drift to the curb. Then Garrett instructed him to stay in the car, while he and Karla went in to case the joint.

Garrett approached the front door with no idea yet of how he was going to break in. He got a grip on the door handle, levered it down and pushed. To his surprise, the door swung inward onto the darkened space beyond.

Dean, they knew, was in the habit of parking his bike indoors, and they soon encountered the machine, standing in the foyer. However, at this point, their plan hit its first snag. Dean had been working on the motorcycle and it was partially disassembled, parts scattered across the space, an open toolbox on the floor, greasy tools scattered hither and yon. A shovel and a pickaxe stood leaning up against the far wall.

It was a problem, but one that was easily overcome. In fact, the revised plan that they hastily put together was even better. They were going to remove the parts of the motorcycle, making it impossible for Jerry Lynn to complete his repairs without dipping deeply into his pocket. Imagine his anger and frustration when he got up in the morning to find half of his Harley missing.

Karla Faye stooped to begin gathering up some of the motorcycle parts. But she'd barely done so when a light came on somewhere in the house and she heard the squeak of a mattress as someone got up from a bed. Then footfalls and Dean's familiar growl, "Who the hell is out there?"

Karla Faye stood poised, ready to flee. Then Danny took the initiative. He snatched up a hammer from the floor and charged towards the bedroom. Karla Faye followed. She saw Danny swing his weapon and strike Dean on the head, then continue his assault, raining down blow after blow on the fallen man.

Karla would later admit that she was thrilled by the brutal attack. She was also frustrated. She wanted to get in on the act, to exact revenge for her friend Shawn. As Danny continued bludgeoning

Jerry Lynn Dean, she noticed that there was someone else in the bed, a woman cowering on the other side, hiding under the covers. Her murderous rage already roused, Karla Faye ran back to the living room to fetch the pickaxe she's seen there. Then she returned to the bedroom and joined in the attack.

She lifted the axe and brought it down on the cowering woman, lifted it and brought it down again. The victim, later identified as 32-year-old Deborah Thornton, screamed only once as Karla Faye, attacked her chest, her legs, her stomach, and shoulders. Twenty-eight blows were delivered, painting the walls of the small room with Deborah's blood.

But still, Karla Faye Tucker's bloodlust was not satiated. She turned her attention towards Jerry Lynn Dean, hacking at his body twenty more times with the axe. Danny then buried the weapon in Deborah Thornton's heart before the two of them walked away from the scene.

It didn't take detectives long to connect the murders to Tucker and Garrett. They'd hardly been discreet about it, bragging to all who would listen. Then, after the police started leaning on witnesses, the whole sordid story came out, with Jimmy Leibrandt the star witness. He'd later turn state's evidence and walk away with immunity for his part in the killings.

Karla Faye Tucker and Danny Garrett were indicted for the murders of Jerry Lynn Dean and Deborah Thornton in September 1983. They were tried separately, but the outcome was the same. Both were found guilty, both sentenced to death.

Danny Garrett would not keep his date with the executioner. He died in prison of liver disease, a short while after his conviction. For Karla Faye Tucker, though, there would be a wait of almost a decade and a half, 14 years during which she went through an ultimately unsuccessful series of appeals. During that time she became a Christian and expressed remorse for her actions, attracting to her cause a number of high-profile backers. It did her no good.

With all other avenues exhausted, a clemency appeal was lodged with the then Texas governor, and future U.S. President, George W. Bush. Bush turned her down.

Karla Faye Tucker was executed by lethal injection on February 3, 1998.

Blood Will Tell

At around 7 o'clock on the evening of November 12, 1983, 15-year-old Lynda Mann left her home in the village of Narborough, to visit a friend. She never returned from that visit. The following morning, her body was discovered on a footpath known as Black Pad. She'd been raped, then strangled to death.

The murder was the first in the history of the quaint Leicestershire community, and as a pall of fear descended on the frightened residents, Detective Inspector Derek Pierce got to work on tracking down the perpetrator. A high sperm count was noted in the semen taken from the victim, suggesting that the killer was aged between 13 and 34. With this in mind, Inspector Pearce compiled a list of likely suspects, many of them residents at the nearby Carlton Hayes mental hospital.

However, despite optimistic predictions of a quick resolution, the investigation soon stalled. Witnesses had reported seeing Lynda in conversation with a young man sporting a punk hairstyle.

However, the police were unable to locate that man, and their blood test initiative also failed to deliver results. All of the suspects tested, including Lynda's stepfather, were cleared. As the investigation faltered and then stalled, the task force that had once comprised 150 officers eventually dwindled to just eight.

Less than ten miles from the murder scene, at Leicester University, a 34-year-old geneticist named Alex Jeffreys was probing the complexities of deoxyribonucleic acid, more commonly known as DNA. Jeffreys had begun his study intent on understanding human evolution, but the tests he conducted were frustrated by the realization that every human's DNA is unique. As a by-product of his research Jeffreys learned that by adding certain enzymes to genetic material, he could produce a pattern, similar to a supermarket barcode. That pattern was consistent whatever the biological material, be it hair, blood, skin tissue, saliva, semen or any other. In March 1985, Jeffreys announced that the chances of any two individuals possessing the same DNA pattern were virtually zero.

On July 15, 1986, 15-year-old Dawn Ashworth entered the Ten Pound Lane footpath, leading from Enderby to nearby Narborough. She was last seen alive at around 5 p.m. Dawn was reported missing later that evening. Her body was discovered in heavy brush at the side of the path on August 2. She had suffered a vicious beating and had then been raped and strangled.

As in the case of Lynda Mann, Dawn had been seen talking to a young man, shortly before she disappeared. In this case, the suspect was a motorcyclist wearing a red helmet and the police soon had him in custody. Richard Buckland worked in the kitchen at the mental hospital. Under sustained interrogation, he confessed to killing Dawn, although he insisted that he'd had nothing to do with the murder of Lynda Mann.

Given the close proximity of the two crime scenes, and the startlingly similar M.O., the police were certain that a single perpetrator had been responsible for both murders. In order to clear things up, they sent semen samples from both victims to Dr. Alex Jeffreys at Leicester University. His response, when it came, left them stunned. A single killer was indeed responsible for the two murders. But it wasn't Richard Buckland. On the eve of his murder trial in November 1986, Buckland, therefore, became the first person ever exonerated of a crime by DNA evidence.

The police, however, were back to square one. Worse still, they knew now that they were hunting a serial killer. In response, a 50-man team was assembled under Inspector Pearce. On January 17, 1987, they announced an ambitious scheme to track down the killer. All males in the region, between the ages of 17 and 34, were to be asked to submit blood and saliva specimens for DNA testing.

The plan was fraught with difficulty. Firstly, it placed the testing lab under huge pressure. Thousands of samples needed to be processed, using what was still a fledgling technology. Second, the testing regimen was open to abuse. Test subjects were required to provide ID, but as driver's licenses in Britain did not include a photograph, it would be easy for anyone to falsify their details. Lastly, subjects were under no legal obligation to comply, although refusal to do so might well arouse police suspicion.

The response to the police request was overwhelming, with over 90% of the identified subjects voluntarily submitting. The results, though, were disappointing. Six months into the operation virtually every person on the list had been tested and the police still did not have a match. Once again, the task force was scaled down, this time to 16.

The police braced themselves, certain that their killer would strike again soon.

On August 1, 1987, a young bakery worker named Ian Kelly was drinking in a pub with some friends. As the drinks began to flow, Kelly started bragging about how he'd helped a work colleague, named Colin Pitchfork, circumvent the police tests. According to Kelly, Pitchfork had asked him to take the test on his behalf, explaining that he thought the police were trying to nail him for some minor sexual offenses. After Kelly agreed, Pitchfork had inserted Kelly's photograph into his passport. Kelly had also practiced forging Pitchfork's signature and had studied Pitchfork's family history, just in case he was questioned.

Kelly's friends thought nothing of his boasts at the time, but as the investigation continued without any signs of a breakthrough one of them went to the police and repeated the story. On September 18, Ian Kelly was arrested at his place of work and charged with conspiracy to pervert the course of justice. He'd later receive an 18-month suspended sentence. That same afternoon, Colin Pitchfork was arrested on suspicion of murder. He soon confessed.

Pitchfork was a married father of two, who worked as a baker and cake decorator. He had a history of sexual perversion and was a compulsive "flasher" who claimed to have exposed himself to over 1, 000 women. Eventually, those compulsions had led him to sexual assault and then to murder. According to his testimony, he received no gratification from the act of murder. He'd killed the two teenagers solely to hide his identity.

Pitchfork was remanded at Castle Court in Leicester on September 21. He was charged with two counts of murder, two counts of indecent assault, and one of kidnapping. The last charge related to another teenager he'd attacked, but who had managed to escape his clutches.

The murder trial of Colin Pitchfork began at Castle Court on January 22, 1988, and concluded that same day. Pitchfork was sentenced to life in prison, with a minimum of 30 years to be served. He later appealed that sentence and had the minimum term reduced by two years. That means he will be eligible for parole in 2016.

The Bodies in the Trunk

Winnie Ruth Judd

George Brooker looked down at the two large steamer trunks before him. It was Monday morning, October 19, 1931, and all of the luggage from the Golden State Limited out of Phoenix, Arizona, had been collected. All except these two. Brooker consulted his list again and ascertained that the two items had indeed arrived at L.A.'s Union Station aboard that train. He decided to wait for a few moments longer before returning them to storage. Someone might still call for them. When they did, Brooker wanted a word.

As a baggage checker, Brooker was under instruction to check any suspicious luggage. This was the era of prohibition, and bootleggers were known to ship illegal hooch via the railroad. But Brooker didn't think that these trunks contained bootleg liquor. From the smell they gave off, and the brownish liquid seeping out of them, he suspected that a hunter was transporting illegally shot venison. He'd seen it done before.

Brooker waited until noon and was just about to send the trunks to storage when he saw a Ford roadster backing up toward the receiving dock. An attractive young woman got out of the car, accompanied by an equally handsome man. The woman pointed to the trunks, then presented Brooker with a baggage claim ticket for both.

While this was going on, Brooker's boss, Jim Anderson, walked over. Brooker had earlier spoken to him about his suspicions, and now Anderson informed the woman that she'd have to open the trunks for inspection before they could be released.

The woman at first appeared flustered, then made a big show of searching in her handbag before declaring that she didn't have the keys. Her husband had them, she said.

Anderson suspected immediately that the woman was lying. Yet, he played along, suggesting that she phone her husband from the station house. The woman then claimed that she couldn't remember his number and she'd have to bring him to the station personally. Without waiting for a response from Anderson, she nudged her companion towards their vehicle. A moment later, they were driving away.

The roadster had barely left when Anderson walked back to his office and called the police. Lieutenant Frank Ryan responded to the call, listened to what Anderson and Brooker had to say and then decided to pick the locks on the cases. Based on the smell, he already had a good idea what to expect. Still, the contents of the trunks caused him to step back and release a sharp breath. Under an upper layer of clothing, the partially decomposed face of a woman stared back at him. Further down were three more pieces of an incomplete female corpse, neatly dissected. That accounted for the smaller trunk. In the larger was the body of another woman, this one left intact.

That discovery had just been made when a janitor made another gruesome find. A beige valise and matching hatbox had been found in the ladies' restroom. The hatbox contained a number of surgical instruments, a bread knife and a Colt .25 automatic. The valise contained the rest of the dismembered corpse. Now the race was on to find the fugitive. The baggage claim ticket told police that her name was Winnie Ruth Judd.

Winnie Ruth McKinnell, known to all as Ruth, was born in Darlington, Indiana, on January 29, 1905. Her father was a Methodist preacher, and she was raised in a strictly religious household. As a teenager, she showed minor signs of the mental instability that was prevalent in the McKinnell bloodline. She became obsessed with the idea of having a baby and accused her boyfriend of getting her pregnant. A subsequent examination proved that she wasn't with child and was, in fact, still a virgin. Then she ran away from home, returning days later to claim that she had been kidnapped and her baby had been stolen from her.

At age 17, Ruth went to work at Indiana State Hospital where she met Dr. William C. Judd, a WWI veteran with a morphine addiction. Judd was besotted with the pretty teenager and although he was 22 years her senior, Winnie returned his affections. They were soon married.

Shortly after the nuptials, Dr. Judd was offered a job as the house physician for a large mining company in Mexico. The couple thus moved there, but it was hardly the glamorous world of travel Ruth's husband had promised her. Still, she could have tolerated the harsh conditions if her husband would only have let her have children like she wanted. Judd refused. The first time Ruth became pregnant, he performed an abortion on her. The second time, she miscarried.

Eventually, Ruth contracted tuberculosis and her husband sent her to a sanatorium in California, while he remained in Mexico. In 1930, she moved to Phoenix, Arizona, hoping the clear desert air might improve her condition.

Her first job in Phoenix was with the wealthy Ford family, whose neighbor, Jack Halloran, soon became a friend. At 44, Halloran was handsome, rich and charming, part owner of Phoenix's largest lumberyard and one of the city's movers and shakers. He was also married with three children. That didn't stop Ruth having an affair with him.

A few months into her employment with the Fords, Ruth was offered a better paying job as a medical secretary at the Grunow Clinic. There she became friends with Anne LeRoi, a 32-year-old X-ray technician, and 24-year-old Hedvig "Sammy" Samuelson. The two women shared a small duplex at 2929 North Second Street, a short drive from Ruth's home on Brill Street. The place soon became a party venue of sorts, with Halloran usually supplying the bootleg liquor and bringing along his married business buddies. Halloran also visited Anne and Sammy on his own, but if Ruth knew about any impropriety, she appeared to turn a blind eye.

In autumn 1931, Ruth moved in with Anne and Sammy for a time, but the arrangement didn't work out. The three were often at each other's throats, ostensibly over housekeeping matters, although the real reason was likely the affections of Jack Halloran. Before long, Ruth returned to her Brill Street apartment. Although her friendship with Anne and Sammy remained intact, the seeds of resentment had been sown. Soon they'd begin to take root.

On Thursday, October 15, Jack told Ruth that he and his buddies were going deer hunting in the White Mountains of northern Arizona. Ruth offered to introduce him to Lucille Moore, a pretty young nurse who worked at the clinic and was from that area. Jack agreed to meet Lucille for dinner at Ruth's house but after picking them up he said that he wanted to stop off at Anne and Sammy's house to say hi to a couple of friends who were visiting there.

While Ruth and Lucille waited in the car, Jack went inside, emerging later with Anne and Sammy in tow. They seemed cordial enough, but as Ruth would later discover they were seething, angry at the idea of Ruth introducing another attractive woman into their circle. Within 24 hours that anger would spill over, bringing matters to a devastating head on the evening of Friday, October 16, 1931.

Nobody but Winnie Ruth Judd knows what happened on that fateful night. What follows is her version of events.

According to Judd, she got home from work around 6:30 p.m. Jack Halloran was supposed to pick her up for dinner but when he

hadn't shown up by nine she realized that she'd been stood up. It
wasn't the first time it had happened and Ruth was angry. She
decided that she didn't want to be there when he eventually did
show, so she hopped a trolley and headed for Anne and Sammy's
house.

All went well at first. The three women sat and talked and then
eventually decided to retire, Anne and Sammy convincing Ruth to
stay the night. But as they sat in their beds and continued their
conversation, the pleasant chitchat turned into an argument.

It started when Anne began criticizing Ruth for introducing Jack
Halloran to Lucille Moore, a woman she claimed had syphilis. Ruth
responded by saying she didn't think it was right to discuss
Moore's medical history. Anne insinuated that Ruth was a tramp
for sleeping with Jack Halloran while she was married. Ruth
countered by calling Anne and Sammy lesbians. Anne then said she
was going to tell Jack that Lucille had syphilis. Ruth said that if she
did, she would make it known that Anne had deliberately damaged
an expensive X-ray machine at the clinic.

Ruth then got up to return a glass to the kitchen, but Sammy
followed her. When she turned, Sammy was right behind her. In
the next moment, Sammy pushed a gun against Ruth's chest.
Thinking she was about to be shot, Ruth fought back. She pushed
Sammy away from her and grabbed a bread knife from the kitchen
counter.

A struggle ensued during which a shot was fired, hitting Ruth in
the hand. Ruth then lashed out with the knife, slashing Sammy

across the shoulder. As the two women rolled on the ground, another shot went off, this time striking Sammy in the chest. Then Anne joined the fray. Armed with an ironing board, she began striking Ruth on the head and exhorting Sammy to, "Shoot her! Shoot her!"

Eventually, Sammy lay still and Ruth, now in control of the gun, staggered to her feet. As Anne continued to beat her with the ironing board, she fired several times. Anne collapsed to the kitchen floor and lay still beside her friend.

With the two women lying dead on the floor, Ruth was filled with the overwhelming need to get out of the house. She dressed quickly and took the trolley back to her apartment. When she arrived, at about 11:30 p.m., Jack Halloran was waiting for her. He was drunk. Ruth told him what had happened then said she was going to phone her husband. Halloran told her not to. He said he would deal with the situation.

She and Halloran drove back to Anne and Sammy's apartment, where they cleaned up the blood on the kitchen floor. Halloran then tried to contact an associate of his, Dr. Brown, to come over and attend to Ruth's hand but was unable to get hold of the doctor. With the crime scene now cleaned, Halloran walked to the garage, returning with a large steamer trunk.

Ruth was by now hysterical and Halloran decided to take her home. He would take care of the rest, he said. He was going to put the bodies into the trunk and then dispose of them in the desert. He told Ruth to take the murder weapon with her.

The following morning, Saturday, Ruth phoned in sick but her employers insisted that she come in. She obliged, spending the day in agony due to the gunshot wound to her hand. At around noon, Halloran phoned and asked her to meet him at Anne and Sammy's house. When she arrived, she was disappointed to see that the steamer trunk was still there. She'd thought that Halloran had already disposed of it.

But Halloran explained that dumping the trunk near Phoenix was a bad idea. If the bodies were found they'd both come under suspicion, especially Ruth who was a known associate of the two women. Instead, he had a new plan. He wanted Ruth to take the trunk to Los Angeles.

Ruth was reluctant, but as Halloran explained his thinking it began to make sense. Her husband and brother were in L.A., so she'd have a perfectly legitimate reason for going there if she were ever questioned. Ruth did, however, have concerns about disposing of the bodies once she got to California. Halloran said it was already taken care of. An associate of his named Wilson would meet her at Union Station and take the trunk off her hands. She was to leave the next day. Halloran would arrange the train ticket.

Eventually, Ruth agreed to the plan. But she had one more question. How had Halloran been able to get both women into the trunk?

"I forced Anne into the bottom of the trunk," Halloran smirked. "Sammy was...operated on. It was the only way to make her fit."

Halloran then left the house in order to arrange Ruth's train ticket, leaving her to await the Lightning Delivery Service, which was going to transport the trunk to the train station.

But here the plan began to go awry. The driver refused to take the trunk, insisting that it was too heavy to be shipped by rail. He suggested that Ruth split the weight between two boxes. Panicked and desperate to get away from the death house, Ruth then asked him to move the box to her apartment. There, she had the gruesome task of transferring Sammy's mutilated remains to other receptacles, a smaller trunk, and a beige valise. She tried to call Halloran for help but was unable to contact him. She was left to deal with the crisis alone.

The following day, Sunday, October 18, Ruth again tried to contact Halloran. When he remained inaccessible, she called on her landlord and his son to help her deliver the trunks to the railroad station. When they commented on the weight of the load, she explained that the boxes contained her husband's medical books. Once at the station, Ruth paid $4.50 in excess baggage fees, then picked up the ticket Halloran had left for her.

As she boarded the train and awaited its departure, Ruth felt relief wash over her. Twelve hours from now she'd be in Los Angeles. Then Halloran's friend, Wilson, would relieve her of the trunks and the whole nightmare would be over.

But no Mr. Wilson was there to meet her in Los Angeles. Halloran had never arranged for him to do so, if indeed, Wilson even existed. Halloran had left her in the lurch. He'd set her up. When she tried to call him, his housekeeper informed her that he had gone hunting and would be unavailable for some time.

Panicked, she'd turned to her brother, Burton McKinnell, to help her collect the trunks, without telling him what they contained. After she was refused access to the luggage, she asked Burton to drop her off in downtown L.A. and promptly disappeared. Now every newspaper in the city carried her picture on its front page under lurid headlines like, "The Trunk Murderess," and "The Blonde Butcher." Now every lawman in the city of Los Angeles was looking for her.

Ruth managed to stay at large until October 23 when she was found hiding out in a funeral parlor. Frightened, half-starved and in pain from the hand wound that had turned gangrenous, she willingly surrendered and was returned to Phoenix, to stand trial for murder.

Right from the start, the Arizona authorities rejected Ruth's version of events, implicating as it did, the powerful and politically connected, Jack Halloran. According to the State of Arizona, the murders had been carried out execution style, Ruth shooting the women in the head while they slept. That was the version they put forward at trial and that was the version that prevailed. Found guilty of first-degree murder in February 1933, Ruth Judd was sentenced to death by hanging.

There are a few problems with the state's version. Firstly, experts who examined the dissection of Sammy Samuelson stated that the person who carried out the cuts had surgical skills. Ruth Judd had no such expertise. Second, it would have been impossible for a frail woman like Ruth to lift the much bigger Anne LeRoi into the trunk. Third, the state asserted that the women were shot as they slept, yet no blood was found in the bedroom. Fourth, the mattresses were missing from the beds (police suggested this was to get rid of blood evidence), but Ruth did not have a car and therefore had no means to transport them. When one of the mattresses was eventually found, miles from the scene, there was no blood on it.

Still, the state prevailed, Winnie Ruth Judd remained on death row until a competency hearing ruled her insane. She was then transferred to the Arizona State Asylum, where she remained until she was eventually paroled on December 22, 1971.

That does not tell the full story. During her period of incarceration, Ruth escaped seven times, usually staying at large for only a few days with each escape. However, on October 8, 1962, she walked out of the front door using a passkey given to her by a sympathetic nurse. This time, she was free for more than six years, ending up in Oakland, California, where she lived under the assumed name Marian Lane. She was eventually recaptured on June 27, 1969. Eighteen months later, the state of Arizona released her.

Ruth returned to California, where she lived in Stockton with her dog, Skeeter. She enjoyed almost three decades of freedom before passing away peacefully in her sleep on October 23, 1998, at the age of 93.

When Games Turn Deadly

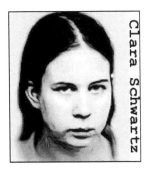

On the rainy Saturday evening of December 8, 2001, a lone car worked its way along a stretch of dirt road in Leesburg, Virginia. Inside were two young men and a young woman and they were here on a mission, they were here to kill the man who'd been tormenting their friend, Clara Schwartz.

Two days later, on Monday, January 10, employees at the Center for Innovative Technology in Herndon, Virginia, were concerned about one of their colleagues. Biophysicist Robert Schwartz was a meticulous and punctual man who seldom, if ever, missed a day of work. Yet the 57-year-old wasn't there today and hadn't called. Neither was he answering his phone. As concern grew, someone phoned one of Schwartz's neighbors in Leesburg and asked that he check on him. The neighbor found Schwartz lying face down on the floor, dried blood caking his numerous stab wounds. A letter 'X' had been carved into the back of his neck.

The first clue in the case wasn't long in coming. Schwartz's neighbors reported a car parked near his house on Saturday night, three people inside. The car had become stuck in the mud and a tow truck had arrived to haul it out. It was a valuable lead and the police soon discovered that the call to the towing company had been made from the Schwartz residence. The operator was also able to tell them who'd placed the call. The man had given his name as Michael Pfohl.

The detectives working the case were at first certain that the name was an alias. I mean, who would be stupid enough to make a phone call from a murder scene using his real name, right? But, as it turned out, the name was genuine. Michael Pfohl, 21, was traced and brought in for questioning. His girlfriend, 19-year-old Katherine Inglis, came with him.

Pfohl and Inglis seemed eager to talk. Yes, they'd been outside the Schwartz house on Saturday night they said, but they hadn't committed the murder, a recent acquaintance of theirs, Kyle Hulbert, had been responsible. Inglis said that she and Pfohl had given Hulbert a ride to the Schwartz home at the request of their friend, Clara Schwartz, the victim's daughter. They'd had no idea what he intended doing there. On arrival, Hulbert got out of the vehicle and walked towards the house. Pfohl then tried to turn the car around so that they'd be pointing in the right direction when Hulbert got back. However, while doing so, he got stuck in the mud.

When Hulbert did returned he was carrying a 27-inch sword that Inglis noticed was covered in a "red liquid." Pfohl asked him to return to the house to phone for a tow truck, but Hulbert refused, saying he was scared to go back in there. It was then, Inglis said, that she realized Hulbert had killed Robert Schwartz.

Having given her story and named Hulbert as the killer, Katherine Inglis naively asked if she was free to go. To her surprise, she and Pfohl were charged with murder and retained in custody. Then the police went looking for Kyle Hulbert. However, one aspect of the case still bothered the investigators, was Clara Schwartz involved in her father's murder, and if so, to what extent?

It wasn't until December 12 that the police brought Clara Schwartz in for questioning. Clara was interrogated for five hours but gave nothing up. She said that she'd only recently met Kyle Hulbert and that she couldn't understand why he'd want to hurt her father. She also denied that she'd asked anyone to drive him to her father's house. With no reason to detain her, the police let her go.

Kyle Hulbert, meanwhile, had offered up a full confession to the murder, insisting that he'd worked alone. According to Hulbert's version of events, he'd met Clara Schwartz at a Renaissance festival in the fall of 2001. The pair had immediately hit it off due to their shared fascination with witchcraft and the occult, and with role-playing computer games. In the course of their conversations, Clara had told him about her abusive father, how he punched her and pulled her hair and was always criticizing her lifestyle and friends. He'd also tried on several occasions to poison her, Clara said. And she was sure that he was going to try again when the family went on a planned vacation to the Virgin Islands.

Hulbert, as the police would discover, was a deeply troubled young man. He had a history of mental disorders and had spent time in several psychiatric institutions for conditions ranging from paranoid schizophrenia to bipolar disorder. He fancied himself a warrior in the make-believe world of dungeons and dragons. He appointed himself as Clara's protector. If Robert Schwartz was trying to hurt Clara, he decided, then Robert Schwartz would have to die.

On the evening of the fateful drive out to Leesburg, Hulbert had carried with him a 27-inch sword, hidden from Pfohl and Inglis. When they arrived at the house, he walked up to the door and knocked. Robert Schwartz answered the door and Hulbert asked if Clara was in. Schwartz said she wasn't but invited Hulbert in when Hulbert asked if he could get Clara's phone number. Hulbert then went to use the bathroom. When he returned, he confronted Schwartz and accused him of abusing Clara.

According to Hulbert, Schwartz didn't deny the allegation. Instead, he smiled and then gave Hulbert a backhand slap, which cut him above the left eye. Hulbert had then drawn his sword and begun slashing and stabbing at Schwartz, not stopping until the man lay bleeding at his feet. He said that before Schwartz died, he'd looked up at him and asked, "What did I ever do to you?" Hulbert then thrust with the sword, delivering the killing blow.

With Schwartz lying dead and bloodied on the ground, Hulbert rinsed off the sword and then turned out the lights. A voice told him to leave quickly because the victim's soul had already departed its body. He then rushed out to join his friends.

The police were prepared to buy most of Hulbert's version of the attack. They were not, however, prepared to accept Hulbert's assertion that he'd acted alone, that Pfohl and Inglis knew nothing about what was about to happen. They were also dubious of Hulbert's claim that Clara Schwartz was innocent in all this. In order to get to the truth, they decided to offer Kathleen Inglis a deal, to turn State's evidence in exchange for a reduced sentence.

Inglis, already shaken up by her brief period of incarceration, was more than happy to cooperate. She admitted that Clara Schwartz had frequently discussed plans to kill her father. Schwartz had told her and Pfohl on several occasions that her father was abusive and had tried to poison her. She'd also spoken about another motive for killing her father. She wanted access to her inheritance and was afraid that her father might cut her out of his will.

Armed with this testimony, the police arrested Clara Schwartz at her dorm at James Madison University, on February 2.

Clara Jane Schwartz was arraigned for murder on February 5, 2002. By then, the police had been able to examine her computer and had discovered a number of coded e-mails and coded messages discussing the murder. In them, she repeated the allegations of abuse and said that her life would be better if her father were dead. Responding to one message where Hulbert asked if he should kill her father, Clara typed: "All I ask is that it is not traced back to me."

It would also emerge that on the night before the murder, Clara sent Hulbert $60 via overnight delivery. She'd later admit that this was for gas to get to the farmhouse and also for rubber gloves, a cap and cleaning cloths to avoid any trace evidence being left at the scene.

Clara Schwartz's trial began in October 2002, ten months after the murder. The defense strategy was to try and shift the blame to Kyle Hulbert. Clara had never asked him to kill her father they said, other than as part of a computer role-playing game. The delusional Hulbert had misinterpreted this and carried out a real murder.

However, this theory was countered by the prosecution, who produced as a witness, Clara's former boyfriend, Patrick House. House said that he too had been asked by Clara to murder her father. At first, she'd framed it within the context of a computer game. But before long she'd made it clear that she wanted the murder carried out in real life. House had then opted out of the relationship. Not long after, Clara had turned to Kyle Hulbert.

Clara Schwartz would eventually be found guilty of murder and sentenced to 48 years in prison. In accordance with Virginia's truth-in-sentencing scheme, she'll have to serve every one of those years and will only be freed in November 2043.

She is currently housed at the Fluvanna Correctional Center for Women, near Troy, Virginia.

Kyle Hulbert pled guilty to first-degree murder in March 2003. He was sentenced to life in prison without the possibility of parole. Michael Pfohl entered a guilty plea to second-degree murder and got 18 years. Katherine Inglis was sentenced to 12 months behind bars. Given the time she'd already spent in prison, she had six more days to serve at the time sentence was passed.

Death In The Sky

On September 9, 1949, a Canadian Pacific Airlines flight took off from Quebec City en route to Baie-Comeau. Forty-one minutes into the flight, over the town of Sault-au-Cochon, at the confluence of the St. Francis and St. Lawrence rivers, the plane exploded. All 23 people on board were killed in the tragedy, which was originally put down to mechanical failure.

However, that finding did not stand up to the scrutiny of air crash investigators. Drs. Jean-Marie Roussel and Robert Péclet, of Montreal's Laboratory of Forensic Medicine, applied an emission spectrograph to the crash debris and made a startling discovery. The debris delivered clear evidence that the plane had been brought down by a bomb. The question was, why?

An examination of the passenger list provided no answers, but there was one irregularity in the cargo manifest, and item that had been taken on board with a fictitious delivery address. Following up on that clue, investigators learned of a mysterious woman in black who had delivered the package to the airport.

The police appealed for information and ten days later they hit paydirt when a taxi driver came forward to say that he had driven a woman, fitting the description, to the airport on the day of the crash. He even remembered where he'd picked her up and passed on the address to the police. When detectives called at the home, they learned that the tenant, Marguerite Pitre, was in hospital, following a failed suicide attempt.

Pitre was tracked to the hospital and soon admitted that she had been the woman who had delivered the package. She'd done it at the behest of a former lover named Albert Guay, she said. It had been part of a plot to murder Guay's wife, Rita Morel, who'd been a passenger on the flight.

Joseph-Albert Guay (commonly known as Albert) was born in Quebec in 1917. He was the youngest of five children, spoiled rotten by his mother, accustomed to getting his own way, and inclined to throw a tantrum if he didn't.

During the war, Guay worked at Canadian Arsenals Limited in St. Malo, Quebec, where he met, and later married, Rita Morel. When the company closed in 1945, he set himself up in a small jewelry and watch repair store in Quebec City.

At first, the Guays appeared to have a happy marriage. But all of that was to change after Rita gave birth to the couple's first child. Albert had carried his juvenile petulance with him into adulthood.

He wasn't prepared to share his wife's affections with a baby. He began casting his eye around and embarked on a string of affairs, none of them lasting very long until he met Marie-Ange Robitaille.

Marie-Ange was just 17 years old and Albert was clearly smitten with her. In order to disguise his marital status, he used the assumed named Roger Angers and under this name, he set Marie-Ange up in a small apartment. Before long, he'd given her a ring and proposed marriage.

His assumed identity might have fooled his naïve young lover, but unfortunately for him, Rita came to hear of the affair. She confronted Marie-Ange who, on hearing that her beau was married promptly ended the affair, leaving Albert seething. While publically he reconciled with his wife, he began plotting to kill her.

Guay, in fact, had another reason for wanting his wife dead. His business was failing, and as the debts began piling up, he took out a $5, 000 insurance policy on Rita's life. Poison was briefly considered as a murder weapon, but then Guay hit on a new idea, a diabolical plan that spared not a thought for the many innocent people he was about to slaughter.

Guay's first step was to commission clockmaker Genereux Ruest, the brother of his former lover, Marguerite Pitre, to build a bomb for him. Some doubt exists as to whether Ruest knew what the bomb was for, but he nonetheless put together the device, using dynamite and a simple timing mechanism made from an alarm clock. Guay next recruited Pitre to deliver the bomb to the airport for him. Then he got to work on convincing his wife to take the flight.

At the time, Guay did a fair amount of air travel around Canada, visiting manufacturers and prospective customers. He began pestering Rita to make one of the trips in his stead and although she was initially reluctant, she eventually agreed. Guay bought the plane ticket himself and drove his wife to the airport. At the last minute, he bought additional travel insurance for Rita, including $10, 000 in life cover.

Joseph Albert-Guay was arrested two weeks after the fatal air crash. Charged with 23 counts of murder, he was put on trial in February 1950. He was found guilty and sentenced to hang, the execution carried out on January 12, 1951. His last words were typically narcissistic. "At least I die famous," he said.

Ruest and Pitre, meanwhile, were both claiming innocence. According to Ruest, Guay had told him that the bomb was to be used for clearing tree stumps from a field; according to Pitre, she thought that the object she was delivering to the airport was a statue. Neither was believed by the jury at their respective trials, not least because Guay insisted that both were willing and informed conspirators.

Genereux Ruest was convicted of murder and put to death on July 25, 1952. Marguerite Pitre, also, was found guilty of murder. She was executed on January 9, 1953, the last woman to be hanged in Canada.

There is an interesting footnote to the story. In 1955, 24-year-old John Gilbert Graham placed a bomb aboard United Airlines Flight 629, out of Denver. The bomb detonated shortly after take-off killing all 44 people on board, including Graham's mother Daisie King, who he had insured for $62, 000. Graham later admitted that he had been inspired by Albert Guay. He was put to death in Colorado's gas chamber on January 11, 1957.

One Night In Hell

In the early hours of July 14, 1966, student nurse Judy Dykton decided to get in some extra studying for an upcoming neurology exam. Sweltering July weather had forced Judy to sleep with her fan on. Now, as she turned it off, she heard what sounded like an animal crying outside. Ignoring it, she headed downstairs to load some laundry into the washer before hitting the books. Returning to her room a few minutes later, she heard the cry again – only this time it sounded like a child. Judy pulled open the blinds and looked to the townhouse across the street, a residence for trainee nurses like herself. There was a woman crouched on a window ledge, who she recognized as Corazon Amurao, a Filipino exchange student. Cora was crying and as Judy opened the window she could make out the frantic woman's words: "Oh my God, they're all dead!"

Snatching her robe, Judy ran across the street to 2319 East 100th Street. As she entered, she saw Gloria Davy, another student, lying face down on a couch. She was nude, her hands tied behind her back, a strip of cloth knotted tightly around her neck, her skin an unearthly bluish color. Judy then fled the building and went back across the street to rouse Mrs. Bisone, the housemother.

By the time the housemother headed to number 2319, in the company of another student, Leona Bonczak, Cora had jumped from the 10-foot ledge and stood shivering on the front stairs. She begged Leona and Mrs. Bisone not to go in, fearing the killer might still be around. Leona pushed past her nonetheless and entered the home. She saw Gloria Davy first, checked her vital signs and determined that she was dead. Then she mounted the stairs to the first floor where she found Patricia Matusek lying half in and half out of the bathroom. She too had been killed. Fighting the urge to run, Leona crept along the corridor and peered into the two bedrooms that served as dormitories for the students. A scene of unprecedented carnage greeted her. Another six young women lay brutally slain, the scene drenched in so much blood that all but one, Nina Schmale, were impossible to recognize.

Numb with shock, Leona returned downstairs where she informed Mrs. Bisone that the girls were dead. Mrs. Bisone then picked up the phone and called South Chicago Community Hospital. When she was asked what had happened, all she could say was: "I need help."

Someone, meanwhile, had flagged down a police officer, a rookie patrolman named Daniel Kelly. Kelly listened somewhat incredulously to the story being relayed to him by an excited babble of voices. Then he entered the house, emerging shortly after, somewhat paler and with his gun drawn. He immediately made a radio call to headquarters.

Joe Cummings, WCFL radio police reporter was monitoring police frequencies at the time and picked up the call. The young police officer making the report sounded frantic, but from what Joe could make out, he was saying that eight young women had been murdered at 2319 East 100th Street. Cummings immediately turned his car around and headed in that direction. Approaching the building he found the street all but deserted. Officer Kelly stood in the road, walking in circles, his uniform disheveled, face ghostly white, in obvious distress.

"What happened here?" Cummings asked.

"It's homicide," was all the cop could say.

Cummings entered the building and immediately saw Gloria Davy. He then headed upstairs. With the sun just now beginning to filter light into the building, he saw the first body. The amount of blood spattering the scene was sickening. There was a bloody handprint on a doorframe, fingerprints clearly visible; blood was spattered on the walls and seeped into the carpet. He could hear it squishing in the rug under his feet. In all his years working the Chicago crime beat, Cummings had never seen such brutality. He barely made it downstairs before throwing up.

One of the first detectives on the scene was Jack Wallenda, a relative of the famous circus trapeze troupe, the Flying Wallendas. The veteran detective had witnessed some brutal homicides in his time, but nothing that prepared him for the carnage that awaited him inside 2319. Slowly, methodically, he began working the scene.

First, there was Gloria Davy, lying belly down on the couch, her hands tied behind her with double knots that looked professional. A strip of sheet was knotted tightly around her neck and there was what appeared to be semen between her buttocks. Upstairs, lay the body of Pamela Wilkening, gagged and stabbed through the heart. Near her, Suzanne Farris, face down in a pool of blood, a white stocking knotted around her neck, 18 stab wounds to her chest and neck.

Next, Mary Ann Jordan, stabbed three times in the chest, once in the neck, and in the eye. In the northwest bedroom, he found Nina Schmale, her nightgown hoisted over her breasts, hands bound, a pattern of stab wounds around her neck. Under a blue cover, lay Valentina Paison, her throat cut from ear to ear. Close by was Merlita Gargullo, stabbed and strangled.

The last body, that of Patricia Matusek, lay in the bathroom. She'd been strangled, her clothing disarranged to display her breasts and vagina. Bruises on her abdomen suggested that the killer had also kicked her in the stomach. Bloody towels lay scattered on the bathroom floor. It was the worst crime scene Wallenda had ever seen.

Cook County Coroner, Andrew Toman, had meanwhile arrived at the death house and begun the gruesome task of examining the bodies before releasing them for transport to the morgue. The house was sealed, crime lab technicians got to work looking for clues, homicide detectives hit the streets determined to catch the monster who had done this.

Armed with a description of the suspect – six feet tall, blond hair, 160 lbs, southern drawl – Detective Wielosinski stopped at a nearby gas station, a known hangout for the area's shady characters. There an attendant told him about a man matching the suspect's description who'd left his bags at the station a couple of days before, complaining about losing out on a job aboard a ship. The man had spoken to the manager, Dick Polo, the attendant said. Wielowski called Polo at home and learned that he'd directed the man to a rooming house on 94th and Commercial. The cops began canvassing the area's many flophouses, certain that they were closing on their man. However, their search turned up nothing.

Wielosinski was now sure that the man they were looking for was a merchant seaman, so he went to Union Hall where an agent told him about an irate seaman who'd lost out on a double booking. The man had had a strong southern drawl, the agent remembered, and he'd jotted his name down on a worksheet. Rummaging through his wastebasket, he fished out a crumpled piece of paper. The name written there was, Richard B. Speck.

Armed now with a name, the police intensified their search. Privately, many of them feared that their suspect had hopped a ship or a freight train and escaped their net, but Richard Speck had done no such thing. In fact, he was less than a mile away, at a dive called Pete's Tap, drinking with an old buddy, William Kirkland.

By mid-morning, the drunken duo had made their way to another bar, Soko-Grad, where they continued drinking. While they were there, word of the massacre reached the patrons and Speck was heard to comment, "It must have been some dirty motherfucker that done it." Late that day, Speck was seen drinking with another acquaintance, Robert R. "Red" Gerald, at the Shipyard Inn.

Wielosinski, meanwhile, had traced Speck's last known telephone number, which turned out to be his sister's home. He arranged for a union agent to call and tell Speck's sister that he had a job for him. The agent spoke to Speck's brother-in-law, Gene Thornton, who tracked Speck to the Shipyard Inn and told him about the job. However, the agent made a crucial error. He said that the assignment was aboard the SS Sinclair Great Lakes. This was the ship on which Speck had lost his previous job offer and he knew that she'd already sailed. Now he also knew that the cops were onto him.

Speck returned immediately to his room, packed his bags and ordered a cab. Giving the cabbie vague directions, he eventually called him to a stop in front of a random building in Cabrini-Green. There, he took a room at the Raleigh Hotel using the name John Stayton.

A while later Speck went out and returned with a black woman who he took up to his room. About a half hour later, the woman came downstairs and told front desk clerk, Algy Lemhart, that Speck had a gun.

The following morning, Lemhart reported the incident to his manager, who called the police. Two officers were dispatched and questioned Speck for about 15 minutes, during which time he revealed his true identity. However, the officers were not aware that Speck was a wanted fugitive. They confiscated the gun, gave him a warning, and left.

Relieved at his narrow escape, Speck hit the bars. That evening found him at the Pink Twist Inn, where he was seen knocking back Jim Beam and cokes. The police meanwhile had tracked him to the Shipyard Inn and learned that he'd left in a Commercial cab. When the cabbie revealed that he'd dropped Speck in Cabrini-Green, officers flooded into that area. They picked up Speck's drinking buddy Red, but still in a drunken stupor, he was unable to provide any clues as to the fugitive's whereabouts.

Speck by this time had hooked up with a couple of winos, Claude "One Eye" Lunsford and "Shorty" Ingram. The winos were staying at the Starr Hotel and Speck quickly went back to the Raleigh, packed his bags, and headed to the Starr, telling Algy Lemhart on the way out that he was, "going to the laundry." A short while after Speck left, two detectives came in and showed Speck's picture to Lemhart. The clerk informed them that they'd missed their man by 15 minutes.

Back at the Starr Hotel, a flophouse where windowless cubicles went for 85 cents a night, Speck and his new drinking partners were sitting on the fire escape, passing a bottle of cheap wine between them. One Eye and Shorty would later say that Speck seemed overly interested in learning how to hop a freight. He spent most of the evening trying to persuade them to show him the ropes. The following morning he continued badgering, but the hoboes said they planned on staying in Chicago a while longer. Giving up, Speck eventually left.

On Saturday, July 19, 1966, word came that the fingerprints found at the townhouse had definitely been matched to Speck. An arrest warrant was duly authorized by Assistant State's Attorney, William J. Martin. The news came as a boost to the physically and emotionally drained officers. It spurred them on to intensify their efforts.

Meanwhile, Speck had sold off some of his belongings to raise money for another drinking binge. Armed with a couple of bottles of cheap wine, he headed for the Starr Hotel to hook up with his new acquaintances. However, on route to the hotel, he saw several newspapers with his name and photo splashed across the front page. Speck went back to the Starr Hotel, downed the wine, smashed the bottle and cut his wrists. He then crept to his buddy One Eye's cubicle and lay on the cot bleeding. Finding him there, someone called an ambulance and he was rushed to Cook County Hospital, the same hospital where his butchered victims now lay.

In the emergency room, a first-year resident named Leroy Smith examined Speck's wounds. While doing so, Smith noticed a tattoo on Speck's forearm, which read: "Born to Raise Hell." Smith recognized the tattoo from a description in the newspaper and was certain that this was the man that the entire Chicago Police force was searching for. He took his suspicions to a policeman who was guarding another patient down the hall. The patrolman came in to view Speck and then made the necessary calls. The search for Chicago's most wanted fugitive was over.

Richard Speck's trial began on April 3, 1967, in Peoria, Illinois, three hours southwest of Chicago. The prosecution team was led by Assistant State's Attorney William Martin, the defense by renowned liberal lawyer, Gerald Getty. Martin had, in fact, applied to work for Getty after he graduated law school, and had been turned down. Now the two met as equally matched adversaries – with a man's life at stake.

From the outset, the defense team's approach was obvious, they intended discrediting the investigative methods that had led to the arrest of Richard Speck. It was a strategy that was always doomed to failure, especially with the prosecution holding their trump card, the sole survivor, Cora Amurao. When Amurao was asked if she could identify the killer of her fellow students, she rose from her seat in the witness box, walked directly across the floor, stopped in front of Speck and pointed at him. "This is the man," she said, in the trial's most dramatic moment.

Cora then went on to describe what had happened on that fateful night. She had been up studying when she heard four knocks at the door of the townhouse at around 11 pm. She went to answer it and encountered Speck, dressed in black, standing in the doorway, a revolver in his hand. He pushed her back into the room and grabbed her arm. "Where are your companions?" he said.

The knocks had also brought Merlita Garguilo to the door. Speck forced both of the women from room to room until he'd roused all of their sleeping colleagues. He then herded all of them into one of the bedrooms and made them sit in a semi-circle, their backs to the window. Speck sat facing them smiling, then said, "I want some money. I'm going to New Orleans." He then allowed each of the nurses, in turn, to fetch their purses and hand over their cash.

While they were doing so, Gloria Davy returned home from a date with her boyfriend. She was slightly tipsy when she staggered into the bedroom and saw Speck with the gun. She tried to scream, but he warned her to be quiet and told her to join the other women. Then he began tearing strips from a bed sheet and tying each woman's hands and feet. He then separated Pamela Wilkening off from the group and took her to another room.

Two other nurses, Mary Ann Jordan and Suzanne Farris, returned from a chat session and opened the door to the back bedroom where they saw Speck hovering over a bound and gagged Pamela. They screamed and tried to run, but Speck cornered them in another room. He stabbed and strangled the women to death, then washed up before returning to Pamela and finishing her off with a single stab to her heart. He washed up again, then returned to the other room where he pulled Nina Schmale from under the bed where she was trying to hide.

In the other bedroom, he raped Nina before killing her by stabbing her in the neck and suffocating her with a pillow. Next, he took Valentina, then Merlita.

Another 30 minutes passed before Cora heard water running. Then Speck returned and carried Patricia Matusek away. Cora heard him ask, "Are you the girl in the yellow dress?"

After raping Patricia in the bathroom, Speck punched her in the stomach, rupturing her liver. Then he strangled her to death.

Speck came back to the room, undressed Gloria and raped her. Cora, hiding under the bed, held her breath and prayed that he wouldn't find her. Eventually, Speck got up from the bed and carried Gloria downstairs. Fearing she'd be found, Cora rolled across the bedroom and found cover under a different bed. Then she waited, fearing that Speck might return at any moment to drag her to her death. Cora stayed hidden until almost 6 a,m. when she crept out onto the window ledge and started screaming.

Cora's testimony was damning and with fingerprints and other forensic evidence providing corroboration, there was only ever going to be one outcome. On April 15, the jury deliberated for only 49 minutes before finding Speck guilty. On June 5, Judge Herbert J. Paschen sentenced him to die in the electric chair.

It was a sentence that would never be carried out. On June 29, 1972, the U.S. Supreme Court declared capital punishment unconstitutional, thus voiding all outstanding death penalties. Speck was given 8 consecutive sentences of 50 to 150 years – effectively 400 to 1,200 years in prison. He'd serve less than 20 of those years.

Richard Speck died in prison of a massive heart attack on December 5, 1991. He was 59 years old. No one claimed his body, and he was cremated, his ashes scattered at an undisclosed location.

The Philadelphia Poison Ring

It started as a routine murder inquiry and ended up uncovering one of the most fiendish murder-for-profit schemes in US history. In January 1939, newly appointed Philadelphia Assistant District Attorney, Vincent McDevitt, was called to his boss's office. The DA, Charles Kelley, had a case for him to handle, the attempted murder of a 38-year-old man named Ferdinando Alfonsi. The information, Kelley explained, had been brought to his attention by the Secret Service, who'd gotten a tip-off from one of their informants. Kelley didn't want to become involved himself because there were rumors that witchcraft was involved and associating his name with such a bizarre case might hurt him politically.

As a rookie in the DA's office, McDevitt did not have the option of choosing his cases, the way DA did. He, therefore, set up a meeting for later that day with the Secret Service agent who'd passed on the tip-off, a man named Landvoight.

According to Landvoight, the tip had been given to him by one of his informants, a man named George Meyer. Meyer ran an upholstery cleaning business, but like so many others, he'd fallen on hard times during the depression. Seeking a way out of his predicament, Meyer had heard from an acquaintance about a man named Herman Petrillo, who was said to provide loans to local businessmen.

At the mention of Petrillo's name, Landvoight said, his ears had pricked up. He'd been tracking Petrillo for years, on suspicion of counterfeiting five and ten dollar bills.

However, the story Meyer had to tell involved not just fake currency, but murder. He said that he'd approached Petrillo for a loan but Petrillo had refused him. Instead, he'd proposed an alternative. He would give Meyer $500 in legal tender and $2,500 in counterfeit bills. In exchange, he wanted Meyer to kill a man named Ferdinando Alfonsi. Petrillo even explained how he wanted the hit carried out. He said that Meyer should club Alfonsi over the head with a length of pipe, then carry him to the top of the stairs and throw him down. That way the police would think the death was an accident.

Meyer had no intention of committing murder. But he feigned interest, hoping Petrillo might offer him an advance. When Petrillo refused to do so, Meyer decided to make a quick buck by selling the information to the Secret Service. Landvoight had then convinced Meyer to continue playing along with Petrillo, hoping that Petrillo would pass him the fake notes and they could nail him for counterfeiting.

In order to carry out the sting on Petrillo, Landvoight allocated one of his agents, Stan Phillips, to work alongside Meyer. A meeting was arranged, with Phillips playing the part of Meyer's friend. Meyer told Petrillo that Phillips had done time for murder. If Petrillo wanted Ferdinando Alfonsi dead, Phillips was the man to do it.

Initially, Petrillo seemed coy about the idea. Then he asked the two men to walk with him to his car. Once inside the vehicle, he opened up, suggesting that they drive Alfonsi to the Jersey shore and drown him, then leave his clothes on the beach to make it look accidental.

Phillips however, was more interested in nabbing Petrillo for counterfeiting than for conspiracy to commit murder. He wanted Petrillo to pass some of his fake bills to them and suggested that Petrillo give then some money to buy a car. They'd then pick up Alfonsi, drive him to a quiet country road, and run him down, leaving his body at the side of the road to make it look like a hit-and-run. Petrillo liked the idea, but wouldn't part with any money for the car. He suggested they steal one.

Over the next few weeks, the negotiations regarding the hit on Alfonsi went back and forth. Eventually, on August 22, 1938, Petrillo summoned the men to a meeting at a diner on Thayer Street. There, he gave them an ultimatum. He was not going to stump up the money for the car. It was up to them to decide. Were they in, or were they out?

Phillips did some quick thinking and tried a different tack. He'd buy the car himself, he said. But in order to do so, he'd have to buy $200 in counterfeit bills from Petrillo. Reluctant at first, Petrillo eventually agreed. He even showed Phillips a sample of his work. Phillips was amazed at the quality. A two-week delivery time was agreed, whereupon the men went their separate ways.

Phillips was overjoyed at the possibility of finally bringing Herman Petrillo to justice. However, as the delivery date arrived and then passed with no sign of Petrillo, he began to worry. Had Petrillo been tipped off?

As Phillips became increasingly concerned, he asked Meyer to check on Petrillo's usual haunts. Unable to find their man in any of those locations, Meyer decided to check on Ferdinando Alfonsi, the man Petrillo wanted killed. He drove to Alfonsi's house and knocked at the door, which was opened by a middle-aged woman. Meyer pretended to be a handyman, interested in doing some maintenance work. He asked to speak to the man of the house and was dismayed to hear that he was grievously ill. Meyer apologized for the intrusion and left.

Phillips was distressed when Meyer told him about Alfonsi's condition. He realized that by focusing on the counterfeiting operation, he'd failed to protect the intended victim of a homicide. He arranged for another agent to check on Alfonsi, posing as an insurance company representative. The report back was not encouraging. Alfonsi, the man said, was paralyzed and in obvious pain. He wasn't able to speak and even had difficulty breathing. Phillips had then passed the information onto Landvoight and Landvoight had called the DA's office. That was how the investigation had landed up in Vincent McDevitt's lap.

But while McDevit was still getting to grips with the case, Petrillo suddenly resurfaced and contacted Meyer. He said that he had the $200 Phillips had asked for and arranged to meet the two of them at a bus stop later that day. There, he handed over an envelope containing forty counterfeit five-dollar bills. However, he said, he no longer needed them to take care of Alfonsi.

"Why is that?" Phillips asked.

"Because he's in the hospital and he ain't coming out," Petrillo grinned.

Ferdinando Alfonsi was indeed in the hospital, and the chances were that he wasn't ever leaving. The unfortunate man was in extreme pain, suffering bouts of projectile vomiting and racked by muscular cramps. A urine test revealed that he'd ingested a large amount of arsenic.

McDevitt then ordered Petrillo arrested for attempted murder. When Alfonsi died a few weeks later, the charge was upped to homicide.

Based on the information McDevitt had received from the Secret Service, he expected that Petrillo would be a tough nut to crack. However, the counterfeiter proved to be exactly the opposite. He began talking right away, minimizing his role and fingering his brother Paul and another associate, Morris Bolber, as the masterminds behind the operation.

McDevitt was confused. "Operation? What exactly are we talking about here, Herman?"

To McDevitt's astonishment, Petrillo began rattling off a list of victims, 70 in all, each of them poisoned in a heinous murder-for-profit scheme.

Investigators now faced the daunting task of proving Petrillo's allegations, a process that would involve exhuming every named victim. However, McDevitt wasn't prepared to wait that long. He already had proof that Ferdinando Alfonsi had been poisoned. He decided to proceed with that case.

On February 2, 1939, the grand jury indicted Herman Petrillo, Paul Petrillo and Stella Alfonsi for the murder of Ferdinando Alfonsi. Herman went on trial a month later, on March 13, 1939. Found guilty, he was sentenced to die in the electric chair.

At the conclusion of the trial, investigators announced plans to exhume 70 bodies and examine them for arsenic. In the meanwhile, Maria Favato, another member of the Philadelphia Poison Ring (as the media was by now calling them), was arrested and quickly confessed to murdering her husband and stepson. Then Herman Petrillo contacted the DA, offering cooperation in exchange for his life. He was politely turned down.

By May 21, 1939, 21 arrests had been made, all of them involving the murder-for-profit scheme. It had also been discovered that Petrillo and Morris Bolber had been running a matrimonial agency. Their M.O. was to find husbands for the women within their circle, insure their lives, and then murder them and claim the insurance payout.

On May 25, 1939, Morris Bolber pled guilty to murder and was sentenced to life imprisonment. Paul Petrillo no doubt hoped for the same treatment when he went on trial in September, but his guilty plea landed him on death row. The last major player in the poison ring, Rose Carina, who was believed to have poisoned three husbands, was found not guilty at her trial.

When the dust eventually settled, 16 men and women had been convicted for involvement in the poison ring, earning sentences that ranged from death to 14 years in prison.

Paul Petrillo was put to death by electrocution on March 31, 1941. His brother, Herman, suffered the same fate on October 20, that same year. Although spared the death penalty, Morris Bolber would never taste freedom again. He died in prison on February 15, 1954, having served 13 years.

Although it was widely reported in the press at the time, there is no evidence that witchcraft played any part in the crimes. The members of the poison ring were motivated only by greed. Their nefarious exploits are believed to have netted them over $100,000 (about $1.6 million in today's value).

Let's Kill Mother

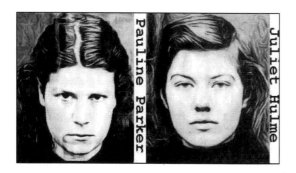

Folie a deaux is a term that was first coined by French psychologists Laseque and Fabret. Loosely translated it means "collective insanity," and in its original interpretation refers to two people who share a common psychotic delusion. These days, though, folie a deaux is more commonly used to describe a bond between two people that brings out the worst in each individual, often leading to criminal acts. Although the phenomenon is quite rare, there are any number of "gruesome twosomes" that fit the bill, from teenaged thrill killers Leopold and Loeb to serial killing partners like Buono and Bianchi, Bittaker and Norris, and Lake and Ng. Another example is a famous case from New Zealand involving two teenaged girls, Pauline Parker and Juliet Hulme.

Pauline Yvonne Parker was born in Christchurch, New Zealand on May 26, 1938. Her father, Herbert Rieper, owned a successful wholesale fish market, her mother Honora Parker, was a homemaker. The couple was never married. When Pauline was a child, she was hospitalized with osteomyelitis, a crippling infection of the bone marrow. It left her with a permanent limp and rendered her incapable of participating in physical activities at school.

Juliet Marion Hulme had also suffered illness as a child. In her case, it was tuberculosis and resulted in her being sent from her home in England to live in the Bahamas, where it was hoped that the warmer weather would have a beneficial effect. Pauline's father was the brilliant physicist, Dr. Henry Rainsford Hulme. Her mother was Hilda Marion Hulme, who was prominent in charity work.

In 1951, Juliet's father was offered the position of Rector at the University of Canterbury. He accepted, bringing his family (which also included Juliet's younger brother, Jonathan) to Christchurch.

The first two years of Juliet's life in New Zealand were spent in and out of hospital. But eventually, when she was 15, she had recovered enough to attend Christchurch Girls' High School, which was where she met Pauline Parker. Initially drawn to each other due to their shared experiences with serious illness as children, the two were soon inseparable.

The friendship was unconventional. Pauline and Juliet began concocting an elaborate fantasy world with their own religion and conventions of morality. They rejected the tenets of Christianity and invented their own saints, based on movie stars and singers of the era. They envisioned their own version of Heaven, which they called The Fourth World. According to their belief system, they could enter into this Fourth World when they reached spiritual enlightenment. That enlightenment was achieved through their friendship.

The girls also made up more down-to-earth fantasies. Both were keen writers and they'd spend hours together coming up with stories, dubbing themselves Gina and Deborah. They'd often sneak out at night to act out their story ideas, eventually concocting a plan to run away to Hollywood, where they believed some movie studio would snap up their stories and make them famous. They even started an orchestrated campaign of shoplifting, hoping to raise money for their trip.

Initially, the two families were pleased about the friendship between the two girls. But as the obsessive nature of the relationship became evident they became concerned. Pauline's mother even sent her to see a psychiatrist, who reported that he believed the pair was engaged in a lesbian relationship. (In later years, Juliet Hulme strongly denied that there was ever anything physical between them).

The chain of events that would eventually lead to murder was set in motion when Juliet's mother started having an affair with a man named Walter Perry, who rented a cottage on their property. Not long after, the Hulme's announced that they were separating, with Henry resigning his post at the university and returning to England, taking Jonathan with him. Juliet was to be sent to relatives in South Africa (ostensibly for her health, but there can be little doubt that her parents saw it as the ideal opportunity to separate her from Pauline).

The girls were distraught at the news. That is, until Juliet flighted a new idea. What if Pauline could come to South Africa with her? Excited at this prospect both girls rushed home to discuss the idea

with their parents. They met with a flat refusal, with Honora
Parker particularly vociferous in opposing the plan.

It is not certain which of the pair first came up with the idea of
killing Honora. The entries from Pauline's diary, which were read
into evidence at the trial, suggest that she was already thinking
along these lines in early 1954. On February 23, she recorded:
"Why could not Mother die? Dozens, thousands of people are
dying. Why not Mother, and Father too? Life is very hard."

But the first mentions of the actual murder appear in June. On June
20, she wrote: "Deborah and I talked for some time. Afterward, we
discussed our plans for moidering Mother and made them clear.
But peculiarly enough, I have no qualms of conscience. Or is it
peculiar? We are so made." (The misspelled word "moider" was
apparently taken from the Brooklyn, New York, pronunciation of
the word "murder").

By June 21 (the day before the murder) the plan was firmly
formulated. "Deborah rang and we decided to use a brick in a
stocking rather than a sandbag. Mother has fallen in with plans
beautifully. Feel quite keyed up."

Then on June 22, which Pauline designated, The Day of the Happy
Event: "I felt very excited last night and sort of night before
Christmas, but I didn't have pleasant dreams. I am about to rise."

June 22, 1954, was a cold winter's day in Auckland, yet Pauline and
Juliet convinced Honora Parker to drive them out to Victoria Park,
on the outskirts of the city. There, the three of them had tea at the

refreshments kiosk before going for a walk along a path. It was 3 p.m., all three of the women wearing coats against the cold.

What Honora didn't know was that both of her companions were carrying a secret. In Juliet's pocket were a handful of pretty, colored pebbles that she'd brought with her. In Juliet's was a half-brick, encased in a sock, making a slingshot.

Juliet skipped on ahead, waited until she rounded a bend and then scattered the pebbles on the path. Meanwhile, Pauline limped along beside her mother. Then, as they reached the spot where Juliet had scattered the pebbles, Pauline drew Honora's attention to them, commenting on how pretty they looked. Honora stooped for a closer look. Pauline withdrew her slingshot and swung it, crashing it against her mother's head.

Honora collapsed to the path. In that moment, Pauline would later recall, part of her wished that she hadn't struck the blow. But another part of her screamed that it was too late, that she was committed, that she had to see this through. She raised the slingshot and struck her mother again, then again. By now, Juliet had run back to join them. She found Pauline on her knees beside Honora's prostrate form, still swinging the bludgeon and delivering blow after blow. She relieved Pauline of the weapon and struck a few blows of her own.

Honora Mary Parker was dead, but the rest of the plan still had to be carried out. With blood dripping from their hands, the girls sprinted the four hundred yards back to the kiosk. "It's Mummy!"

Pauline screamed as she entered the restaurant. "She's terrible! I think she's dead."

"She's covered in blood!" Juliet added hysterically.

Agnes Ritchie, the proprietor of the kiosk, to whom they'd just delivered this startling news, looked back at the girl's and noticed they were covered in blood.

"We were coming back along the track. Mummy tripped on a plank and hit her head when she landed," Pauline continued.

By now, Mrs. Ritchie had summoned her husband, Kenneth. While he ran back down the path to discover the battered body of Honora Parker, the girls went to wash up in the bathroom. Mrs. Ritchie would later testify that she heard them laughing hysterically in there.

Moments later Kenneth Ritchie returned to the kiosk and called the police. When they arrived, Honora's body was removed to the morgue. Detectives then started questioning Pauline and Juliet and it was immediately clear that their ludicrous story didn't hold up. According to them, Honora had fallen and struck her head. How then did they explain the forty-five depressions to her skull? How did they explain the bloody slingshot found in nearby bushes? How did they explain Pauline's diary, carrying as it did their plans for the slaughter of her mother? In short order, Pauline and Juliet found themselves under arrest for murder.

The trial of Pauline Parker and Juliet Hulme took place in Christchurch during August 1954. Their defense counsel tried to have them declared insane but the jury rejected that ploy, finding them guilty of murder on August 28.

Due to their ages, they were ineligible for the death penalty and were ordered detained "at Her Majesty's pleasure." In each of their cases, that amounted to prison time of just five years.

After her release, Pauline Parker gained a B.A. degree from Auckland University and worked for a time as a librarian in Wellington. She later moved to England where she currently lives in Kent and runs a horse riding school for children.

Juliet Hulme also returned to England and went on to have a successful career as a writer, publishing over 50 crime novels under the name Ann Perry.

The Colorado Cannibal

The story of Alfred G. Packer, the so-called "Colorado Cannibal," is one of the most controversial from the Old West. That Packer was a cannibal has never been in doubt. The question is whether he was a murderer. Packer claimed in various confessions that he wasn't, the evidence suggests that he might not have been entirely honest. You be the judge.

Alfred Packer was born in Allegheny County, Pennsylvania, on November 21, 1842. As a young man, he worked as a cobbler, but with the outbreak of the Civil War, he enlisted in the Union Army. Accepted for duty on April 22, 1862, he was honorably discharged just seven months later, when it was discovered that he suffered from epilepsy. He then made his way west, intent on making his fortune in the Colorado gold mines.

In late 1873, Packer, then 31 years old, was hired by a group of some 20 prospectors to guide them from Bingham Canyon, Utah, to the goldfields in Colorado's San Juan Mountains. The party was soon in trouble after much of their food supply was lost when a raft broke loose during a river crossing. Nonetheless, they made it as far as Chief Ouray's Ute camp near Montrose, arriving there in January 1874.

The chief strongly urged them to wait until the spring before they continued their journey. However, a few of the prospectors were keen to reach the goldfields and decided to ignore the advice. The group, comprising Alfred Packer, Shannon Wilson Bell, Israel Swan, James Humphrey, Frank Miller, and the teenager George "California" Noon, set out on February 9. They carried with them a ten-day supply of food, enough they thought, for the 40-mile journey. Unfortunately, the information they had was incorrect. Their destination was 75 miles away, not 40.

Two months later, on April 16, Albert Packer walked into the Los Piños Indian Agency on Cochetopa Creek near Saguache and Gunnison. He appeared hale and hearty and was carrying with him several wallets from which he pulled handfuls of bills to pay for whiskey. When he was asked about the whereabouts of the other men, he seemed surprised. They'd been ahead of him, he said, as he'd hurt his leg and had fallen behind.

But the other prospectors had not made it into town and the more the saloon patrons listened to Packer's story, the more they became convinced that Packer had killed and robbed his companions. Packer denied this outright and continued to deny it even after an Indian scout found chunks of human flesh scattered along the trail he'd walked.

Then, a month after he'd emerged from the wilderness, Packer eventually decided to come clean. On May 8, he gave a confession to General Charles Adams at the Los Piños Agency.

According to Packer's account, the party had become lost and had run out of supplies. Then, as the conditions continued to worsen, Israel Swan, oldest of the group at 65, had died. The others, desperately hungry and unable to see another way out of their predicament had decided to eat him. Four days later, James Humphrey had died and was also eaten. Packer admitted to taking $133 from Humphrey's wallet, as "he wasn't going to need it any longer."

The third to go was Frank Miller, who died in some kind of "accident." Packer didn't elaborate on what the accident was. According to him, he'd been out collecting firewood when it happened. Packer wasn't present when George Noon died either. He'd been out hunting for several days, he said. When he returned, he found that Shannon Bell had shot Noon. That left just Packer and Bell, and by Packer's account, Bell had by now gone crazy. He'd attacked Packer the minute he'd walked into the camp. Forced to defend himself, Packer had killed the madman.

Packer's story sounded feasible, but in order to prove its veracity, the bodies needed to be recovered. A search party was therefore dispatched, with a somewhat reluctant Packer acting as guide. They found nothing, leading them to suspect that Packer's story was a lie. On the search party's return, Packer was arrested and placed in the jailhouse at Saguache on suspicion of murder.

And there would soon be proof that Packer had indeed lied. In August 1874, John A. Randolph, an artist working for Harper's Weekly Magazine, was crossing Slumgullion Pass when he came upon five human corpses, clustered together. Realizing that these must be the missing prospectors, Randolph quickly got out his pad and pencils and sketched the scene. He then hurried on to Saguache, to report his find.

A party of twenty men, including Hinsdale County coroner, W. F. Ryan, set out immediately for the site. Wild animals and the elements had taken their toll on the corpses but it was immediately clear that Packer's account was a lie. The bodies were close together, not scattered along the trail as he'd described. It was also clear that there had been post-mortem mutilations to the corpses. One was missing a head, others had chunks of flesh hacked from them. One appeared to have put up a fight.

But were these really the missing prospectors? A member of the original search party was found and identified each of them. By process of elimination, it was decided that the headless corpse was Frank Miller. The bodies were buried on a bluff overlooking the scene of their demise, an area that would become known as "Dead Man's Gulch."

Having completed the burials, the party departed for Saguache, intent on confronting Alfred Packer with his obvious lies. They arrived to find that he'd escaped the jail and fled. He'd remain at large for nine years.

In March 1883, a man named Frenchy Cabizon, who'd been a member of the original prospecting party out of Utah, walked into a saloon in Fort Fetterman, Wyoming. A familiar booming laugh arrested his attention and as Cabizon turned towards its source he was amazed to find himself face-to-face with the fugitive Alfred Packer. Arrested on the spot, Packer (who had been living under the alias John Schwartze) was hauled before a grand jury, which returned five indictments of murder against him. On March 16, 1883, Packer offered a revised confession, again under the supervision of General Adams.

According to Packer's new account, the party had encountered a severe snowstorm within days of leaving Chief Ouray's camp. By the fourth day, their provisions were running low; by day ten, they were surviving on pine gum. Some in the party, especially Shannon Bell, were being driven to madness by their hunger.

Packer was the official scout of the group, so Israel Swan asked him to climb to the top of a nearby peak, to see if he could find a route for them. Packer had done so, taking several days, but he'd been unable to find a way. He'd then returned to the camp, where he'd found Bell squatting by the fire roasting a large chunk of meat. Nearby lay the corpse of Frank Miller and it was obvious where the meat had come from. The other three men were lying close to the fire, their heads caved in by blows from a hatchet.

As Packer approached the fire, Bell picked up the bloody hatchet and attacked him. Packer fired his rifle, hitting Bell in the stomach. Then, as Bell slumped to the ground, Packer snatched the hatchet away and struck him on the head.

Over the days that followed, Packer tried several times to leave the camp, but each time was driven back by fresh snow flurries. Eventually, driven by his desperate hunger, he'd eaten some of the flesh that Bell had carved from the corpses. He'd managed to survive this way for two months until the snow thawed. Then he'd made his way to the Los Piños Agency, carrying with him a pistol and $70 he had taken from the dead men.

Alfred Packer went on trial on April 6, 1883, at the Hinsdale County Courthouse in Lake City, Colorado. He was charged only with the murder of Israel Swan, as Swan's body showed evidence that he'd tried to defend himself, negating Packer's attempts to claim self-defense.

Packer, himself, testified for over two hours, but his testimony was peppered with lies and inaccuracies, many of which contradicted his sworn confession. It was unsurprising therefore that the jury found him guilty of murder.

One of the legends that have sprung up around this case regards the words used by Judge Melville B. Gerry in delivering his judgment. A popular, and widely believed, version goes something like this: "Alfred Packer, you voracious man-eating son of a bitch, there was only seven registered Democrats in Hinsdale County, and you've gone and eaten five of them. I sentence you to be hanged by the neck until you are dead, dead, dead. I would sentence you to hell if I could but the statutes forbid it."

In truth, Judge Gerry said nothing of the sort. He did, however, sentence Alfred Packer to death.

The date set for Packer's execution was May 19, 1883, but in another twist to this already convoluted case, the judgment would be thrown out on a technicality. At the time that Packer committed his crimes, Colorado had not yet attained statehood. It was therefore determined that the newly incorporated State of Colorado could not try Packer for murder. A new trial was ordered. The charge now was five counts of voluntary manslaughter. Found guilty, Alfred Packer was sentenced to 40 years in jail, eight years for each of his five victims.

But Packer still had one more version of his story to tell. On August 7, 1897, he addressed a letter to the Denver Rocky Mountain News, offering yet another account of what had happened on that snowbound mountain pass.

He now claimed that their provisions had lasted nine days, after which they were forced into boiling and eating their rawhide moccasins, and wrapping blankets around their feet to serve as footwear.

At some point, Shannon Bell became deranged by hunger and everyone else in the party grew afraid of him. Eventually, they reached the Gunnison River and set up camp there. In the morning, Packer went scouting for signs of civilization. When he returned, he found that Bell had killed the others. He then killed Bell in self-defense.

Packer had stayed at the camp for some time, surviving off the flesh of his dead companions. Eventually, he left, wandering blindly through the wilderness until he stumbled into the agency. Somehow, he'd traveled 40 miles without even realizing it.

According to this version of Packer's story, he'd been under medical care for three weeks after reaching the agency. This is a lie. Those who encountered Packer shortly after his arrival, speak of him drinking in the saloon and looking surprisingly well fed for someone who'd spent months in the wilderness.

Packer would spend 16 years in prison before his eventual parole in 1901. By then, he was suffering from Bright's Disease, and the early release was granted on medical grounds. He spent the last five years of his life in Deer Creek Canyon, Colorado, where he was well loved by the local children for the tales of adventure he enjoyed telling. Apparently, he became a vegetarian.

In late 1906, Packer was found unconscious a mile from his home, having suffered a stroke. He spent the last few months of his life in the care of a Mrs. Van Alstine and died on April 24, 1907.

In the years since his death, Albert Packer has become something of a folk hero, with many believing in his innocence. However, an event that occurred in 1989 cast fresh doubt on that belief.

James E. Starrs, a law professor at George Washington University, obtained permission to examine the remains of Packer's five victims. The subsequent excavation was carried out in July 1989 and conducted with all the rigor of an   archaeological dig. The findings were enlightening.

Three of the bodies had blunt force trauma to their heads, as well as cuts to the arms and hands, which were interpreted as defensive wounds. There were also nicks and cuts to the skeletons, which Starrs believed had been made when flesh was hacked from the bodies. Based on this evidence, Starrs concluded that Packer had been lying all along and had indeed killed and eaten his traveling companions.

On the other hand, Starrs findings might actually support Packer's story, and paint Shannon Wilson Bell as the villain of the piece. We shall never know for certain.

An American Tragedy

There was nothing particularly unusual about the young couple that approached Robert Morrison on the morning of July 11, 1906. The young man was dapper and handsome, his female companion prim and pretty. They wanted to hire a rowboat to go out on Big Moose Lake, which wasn't unusual either. Morrison, who made his living hiring such conveyances to tourists, quickly pulled a boat from his shed and sent them on their way. He did think it odd that the man was carrying a suitcase and a tennis racket, but he shrugged that off. It was none of his business.

For most of the morning and into the afternoon, the young couple stayed out on the lake, only coming ashore once, to enjoy a picnic. Other boaters would later recall seeing them out on the water, generally keeping their distance. Then as the day drifted towards evening, they seemed to have disappeared. When they didn't return the boat that evening, nor by the next morning, Morrison began to become concerned, not so much for his craft as for the safety of its passengers. Gathering up a few volunteers he set out onto the lake in his steamer. It didn't take him long to find the missing rowboat.

It was floating, overturned in the water, and Morrison immediately headed towards it, while the rest of the crew scanned the surrounding area. One of them, a young boy, pointed out something below the surface, but the others dismissed the object as garbage. The boy, however, persisted. One of the crew then fetched a long, spiked pole and poked at the object before hauling it up. The crew was stunned when the head and upper torso of a young woman broke the surface of the water.

The rescuers quickly dragged the corpse on board the steamboat, noticing as they did, the terrible lacerations the woman had suffered to her forehead and face. They then spent some time peering into the depths on either side of the steamer, trying to find the woman's companion. Unable to do so, they headed for shore and reported the matter to the police.

It was soon determined that the woman was Grace Brown of South Otselic, New York and that her male companion was Carl Grahm of Albany. Further investigation found that Miss Brown had been employed at the Gillette Skirt Factory in Cortland, New York. No one there had ever heard of "Carl Grahm." Miss Brown's frequent companion, they said, was Chester Gillette, nephew of the factory owner.

Chester Gillette was born in 1883 in Montana. His parents were both members of the Salvation Army and thus his upbringing was one of constant upheaval, as he accompanied his parents on missions to Washington, Oregon, Wyoming, California, and Hawaii. As he grew older, his parents determined that he should have a proper education, which had not been possible due to their frequent moves. They, however, had given up all of their money and worldly possessions when they'd joined the Salvation Army, so Chester's wealthy uncle stepped in. Noah Horace Gillette was the proprietor of the Gillette Skirt Company. His patronage allowed the young man to attend the prestigious Oberlin College in Ohio.

Chester was a bright, but less than diligent, student. He spent two years at Oberlin, dropping out in 1903 to work at various menial jobs. He was employed as a railway brakeman in 1905 when his Uncle Noah again stepped in, offering him a job at his factory in Cortland.

It was at Cortland that Chester first met Grace Brown. A farmer's daughter from a remote area of New York state, Grace had come to Cortland to live with her older sister Ada. She'd found work on the production line at the Gillette Skirt Factory a few months before Chester started there. Although it is not known how they met, the two were seen regularly together by the summer of 1905. Correspondence that passed between them has Chester expressing his deep affection for Grace.

But love letters notwithstanding, Grace Brown was not the only woman Chester was seeing. He was a handsome young man on an upward trajectory with a rich uncle as a patron. Women were attracted to him and he took full advantage, something that distressed Grace whenever news of his dalliances reached her. She remained devoted to him, though. So much so, that in the spring of 1906, she became pregnant with his child.

The pregnancy placed Grace in a dreadful predicament. This was an era when unwed mothers were treated as pariahs within polite society, when to become pregnant out of wedlock was to attract shame to oneself and one's family. She pressed Chester for action, but Chester dithered, as though he expected the problem to somehow resolve itself. The letters that passed between them during this time show Grace becoming increasingly desperate, while Chester seems to be trying to end the relationship, even admitting that he'd been seeing other women.

Grace Brown, however, was a determined woman. In early 1906, she returned from her parent's home to Cortland and again began pressing Chester for a decision. He continued to waver, vaguely suggesting that they could maybe take a trip together in the summer.

But as the months wore on and Grace's condition began to show, Chester was no closer to taking responsibility for his unborn child. Eventually, Grace wrote a letter suggesting that if Chester did not resolve the issue, the world would know that he was the father of her child. Her life would be ruined, but so too would his.

Eventually, Chester relented and agreed to meet Grace in the small town of DeRuyter, New York, on July 9. Grace was delighted at the news. She hoped that Chester had finally come to his senses and would agree that they should be married. Chester had other ideas.

Gillette got to DeRuyter on the evening of July 8, checking in at a local hotel under the name, "Charles George." When Grace arrived the following morning, the two boarded a train for Utica, where Gillette registered them at a hotel as, "Charles Gordon and wife."

The next morning, Gillette handed in some of his clothes at a local laundry and asked for them to be sent on to him at Old Forge. He used his real name for this transaction. Then he skipped out of his Utica hotel without paying the bill, secure in the knowledge that "Charles Gordon" couldn't be traced.

The couple's next stop was Tupper Lake Village, where Gillette reverted to the alias "Charles George." He sent a postcard from this location, asking the paymaster at the Gillette Skirt Factory to forward $5 of his wages to Eagle Bay, New York, where he'd collect it.

By now, Grace's hope that Gillette had invited her on the trip with the purpose of proposing marriage lay in tatters. On the morning of Wednesday, July 11, she broke down during breakfast at the hotel, crying so pitifully that she had to be helped from the dining room by one of the waitresses.

Later that day, she left with Gillette for Old Forge, although he'd convinced her in the interim that they should stop off en route at Big Moose Lake, where they could spend the day picnicking. Although the plan was to stay that night in Old Forge, Gillette registered at the lakefront Glenmore Hotel. This time, he used the name, "Carl Grahm of Albany, New York," but gave Grace's real name and her family's hometown of South Ostelic. With the registration completed, he set off with Grace to the lake. For some reason, he was carrying his suitcase and tennis racket.

No one knows what happened out on the lake or in the hours after Grace's body hit the water. What is known is that, during the night of July 11, a man walked into the foyer of the Arrowhead Hotel in the small town of Inlet, on the far shore of Big Moose Lake. He was carrying a suitcase and his clothes and hair were somewhat damp. He asked about the availability of a room and then registered under the name of Chester Gillette.

By Saturday, July 14, Grace's death had been reported in the papers and the coroner had issued a preliminary report on her death, one that did not sit well with District Attorney George W. Ward. Ward suspected foul play and was determined to track down the mysterious "Carl Grahm," who'd been registered at the Glenmore Hotel with Miss Brown. With this goal in mind, he gathered his team and headed for Big Moose Lake.

By coincidence, an employee of the Gillette Skirt Company, Bert Gross, was at Utica station when Ward arrived there with his entourage. Gross had read about Grace's death in the newspaper and was concerned that Chester Gillette might also have come to harm. He approached Ward and asked if there was any word on Gillette. He then gave Ward a physical description of Gillette, one that closely matched the known facts about "Carl Grahm." Ward then asked Gross if he knew where Gillette might be and Gross mentioned the request for $5 to be sent to him at Eagle Bay.

Ward immediately rushed his men to Eagle Bay. But a search of the town's few hotels produced no result. Gillette wasn't there. Neither had he collected his $5 check from the post office. He had, however, left a message, asking the postmaster to forward his mail to the Arrowhead Hotel in Inlet. He was arrested there the following day.

Gillette initially denied that he'd been the man who'd gone out on Big Moose Lake with Grace. However, once the police turned up the letters between him and Grace, which provided him with a clear motive, he admitted that they'd been together. He still denied murder, though. According to him, Grace had drowned accidentally after falling into the water.

Ward didn't buy it. He believed that Gillette had rendered Grace unconscious with his tennis racket, then pushed her overboard. Gillette vigorously denied this allegation but admitted he'd buried the tennis racket "somewhere in the woods," because he'd thought the police might reach exactly the conclusion Ward was now presenting.

Chester Gillette went on trial at Herkimer County Courthouse on November 12, 1906. The prosecution case was strong, if circumstantial, based mainly on motive, Gillette's suspicious behavior prior to the murder, and his nonchalant attitude after Grace's death became public knowledge. Gillette, his wealthy uncle having by now disowned him, was represented by the public defender.

When Gillette eventually took the stand, he said that Grace had been desperate over the pregnancy and had thrown herself into the water. He had tried to save her but was unable to do so, so he'd swum for shore. He'd then realized that the drowning put him in an awkward position and had decided not to report it. He'd headed for Inlet, burying the tennis racket, which he thought might be used to incriminate him, on the way.

Gillette's version of events sounded farfetched and the jury wasn't prepared to accept it. On December 4, 1906, after just six hours of deliberation, they returned their verdict, guilty as charged. Chester Gillette was condemned to die in New York's electric chair.

Gillette would eventually keep that date with the executioner on the morning of March 30, 1908. He died still maintaining his innocence.

The Sadistic Mr. Heath

Like most psychopaths, Neville Heath displayed signs of his abnormal persona early in life. Born in Ilford, Essex on June 6, 1917, he did poorly at school and gained a reputation for dishonesty. Later, he became an office errand boy, then joined the RAF where his brushes with authority continued. He was charged variously with car theft, fraud and being absent without leave, leading eventually to his dishonorable discharge from the service in September 1937. A year later, he was back in trouble, this time for stealing jewelry from a friend. Sentenced to three years on that charge, he emerged in 1940, whereupon he joined the army.

Heath was posted to the Middle East and for a time he appeared to have turned over a new leaf. He even earned an officer's commission. But the old Neville Heath soon emerged. After he was accused of check fraud, he again absconded, this time fleeing to South Africa, where he enlisted in the South African Air Force under an assumed name.

Heath managed to keep himself out of trouble in South Africa and became such a competent pilot that he was seconded to the RAF in 1944. He flew several missions over Holland in the closing months of the war before returning to South Africa in 1945.

Heath had planned to stay on in South Africa. But after he was court marshaled for wearing decorations he hadn't earned, he quit the Air Force and returned to England, where he went to live with his parents in Wimbledon.

In March 1946, the staff of the Pembridge Court Hotel in Notting Hill Gate, London, were alerted by the screams of a woman, coming from one of the rooms. Entering the suite, they found 32-year-old Margery Gardner tied naked to the bed. Gardner had checked into the hotel in the company of Neville Heath, but despite her obvious distress, she ignored the hotel manager's urgings to press charges.

About a month later, on Saturday, June 15, 1946, a young woman named Yvonne Symonds met a dashing Air Force officer at a dance in Chelsea. The man identified himself as Lt. Colonel Neville Heath and although Yvonne was 10 years his junior, she was instantly smitten.

They went on from the dance to the Panama Club in South Kensington, then later to the Overseas Club, parting only after making plans to meet up the following day.

The couple spent the whole of the next day together and despite their short acquaintanceship, Heath proposed marriage and

Yvonne accepted. They stayed that night together at the Pembridge Court Hotel.

The next few days passed in a whirlwind for Yvonne, as her handsome fiancée phoned several times to restate his undying love and devotion. Unbeknownst to Yvonne, she was not the only woman her future husband was calling. He was also in contact with Margery Gardner, the woman he'd left tied up at the Pembridge Court Hotel. Despite the way her previous encounter with Heath had ended, she agreed to meet him again on Thursday, June 20.

They spent that evening together at the Panama Club, returning to the Pembridge Court Hotel slightly the worse for wear in the early hours.

The following morning, the chambermaid knocked at the door of the room they'd shared. Getting no reply, she used a passkey to enter. She immediately wished she hadn't.

Margery Gardner was lying on her back, on one of the single beds in the room. She was naked and her ankles were bound with a handkerchief. Her face was severely bruised and there were numerous bite and slash marks on her body. One of the bites had all but severed her nipple. An object had been inserted into her vagina. The coroner would later determine that she'd been suffocated, however, that had only occurred after the horrific injuries were inflicted.

On June 22, two days after the murder, Heath took a train to Worthing to visit his fiancée. There he casually mentioned a murder that had happened at the hotel where he'd been staying. Later, he confessed to Yvonne that the victim was an old friend and that he'd given her his room key so that she could carry on a liaison with a lover in his room.

The following day, the papers carried a story about the murder, which named Heath as a 'person of interest' whom the police were keen to interview. Yvonne then phoned Heath and urged him to contact the authorities to clear his name. Heath promised her that he would do so.

Yvonne probably expected that Heath would telephone the police. Instead, he wrote a letter to Inspector Barrett, the officer leading the investigation. In it, he repeated the story he'd given Yvonne. He said that he'd given Margery Gardner his room key so that she could meet up with a lover of hers named, 'Jack.' He had returned to his room at around 2 a.m. and found Margery dead. Panicked, he'd packed up his things and left.

Heath meanwhile had fled to Bournemouth, on England's south coast. There, he checked in at the Tollard Royal Hotel, under the name Group Captain Rupert Brooke.

On Wednesday, July 3, ten days after his arrival in Bournemouth, he met 21-year-old Doreen Marshall, who'd come to the coast to recuperate from a bout of influenza. Heath had soon charmed the young lady into having dinner with him at the Tollard Royal. At around 11:30, the couple left the hotel together, Heath gallantly walking his dinner date back to the nearby Norfolk Hotel, where she was staying.

On Friday, July 5, the manager of the Norfolk Hotel contacted the police regarding one of his guests, who appeared to be missing. A search was carried out during which the registries of all local hotels were checked. On hearing of the inquiries, the manager of the Tollard Royal approached 'Group Captain Brooke,' and asked him about the young lady he'd dined with. Had it not been the missing girl? Heath denied this, insisting that his dinner guest had been an old acquaintance.

The manager suggested that Heath contact the police to clarify the matter, which he agreed to do.

Heath called the Bournemouth police at around 3:30 p.m. and was asked to come down to the station to look at a photograph of the missing girl. He arrived some two hours later, inspected the photo and declared that he'd never met Doreen Marshall in his life.

However, the officer conducting the interview, DC Souter, was suspicious. He thought that 'Group Captain Brooke' bore a striking resemblance to Neville Heath, currently sought by police for questioning regarding the death of Margery Gardner.

Souter took the matter to his superiors, but when they confronted Heath he insisted that his name was Rupert Brook. The police then searched Heath and found in his possession a single pearl, similar to one from a necklace Doreen had been wearing on the night she disappeared. They also found a return train ticket to London and a left luggage token from the local railway station.

The token was for a suitcase. In it, the police found various clothing items labeled with the name, 'Heath.' They also found a woman's hat and scarf, stained with blood that would later be matched to Margery Gardner. In addition, there was a leather riding crop with a cross-weave pattern that matched the injuries inflicted on Ms. Gardner.

Heath was taken into custody and questioned about his involvement in the death of Margery Gardner and the disappearance of Doreen Marshall. He eventually admitted his true identity, although he steadfastly denied any wrongdoing.

The following day, a young woman was walking her dog in Branksome Dene Chine. As she passed a clump of bushes she noticed a large swarm of flies hovering in the air. This struck her as unusual, so she mentioned it to her father when she returned home. At around 8 o'clock that evening, the man decided to check it out for himself and discovered the battered corpse of Doreen Marshall.

The body was naked and it appeared that she had been bound and then battered on the head with a blunt object. There were numerous bite marks, one of which had severed her nipple. In addition, there were knife wounds, two deep cuts to the throat and a Y-shaped cut that ran from each nipple, met in the middle of the torso and then ran down her midriff towards the vaginal region. As in the case of Margery Gardner, an object had been inserted into the vagina. In this case, there was another indignity, something inserted into the anus as well.

Heath was returned to London, where he was charged with the murders of both women. However, by the time the matter came to court at the Old Bailey, on September 24, the prosecution had decided to bring charges only for the murder of Margery Gardner.

Heath's defense counsel sought to have him declared legally insane and produced the eminent psychiatrist, Dr. William Henry De Bargue Hubert to testify to that diagnosis. The jury was unconvinced. They returned a guilty verdict and the judge duly sentenced Heath to death.

Neville Heath was hanged at Pentonville Prison on October 26, 1946. His last request was for a shot of whiskey. "In the circumstances," he added. "You might as well make that a double."

Lessons in Murder

Just after 10 p.m. on Tuesday, May 1, 1990, 23-year-old Pam Smart pulled her Honda CRX to a stop in front of her condo on Misty Morning Drive in Derry, New Hampshire. Pam was late coming home that evening, having attended an after-hours meeting at her job. She got out of her vehicle and walked past her husband's Toyota pickup, then climbed the stairs to the porch. The lights were out, which was unusual. Greg usually left the foyer light on when he got home before her. Nonetheless, Pam unlocked the front door, stepped inside and turned on the lights. In the next moment, she was screaming, running from the house, banging on her neighbors' doors.

"Help! My husband!" Pam shrieked, as doors began to be thrown open. "He's hurt! He's on the floor! I don't know what's wrong with him!"

By now, at least six neighbors had exited their units to see what the commotion was about. One of them had called 911; another, Art Hughes, was trying to calm Pam down, trying to find out what had happened.

"My husband's on the floor," was all Pam would say.

Hughes then ran towards Pam's unit, 4E. Ignoring her warning that there might still be someone in there, he pushed open the door and looked inside. A man lay facedown on the carpet. He wasn't moving. There was blood, a lot of blood.

By now, both the police and ambulance service had responded to the 911 call. But there was nothing they could do for Greg Smart. An officer from the New Hampshire Medical Examiner's office made it official at 11:19. Smart was dead, killed by a bullet to the head. The yellow tape was rolled out sealing off the   crime scene. Now the investigation would begin, the case assigned to Detectives Daniel Pelletier and Barry Charewicz.

Murders were a rarity in the quiet hamlet of Derry, New Hampshire. In the year of the Smart case, Greg Smart was the only homicide victim in the town. Even so, the investigators knew a set-up job when they saw one. The murder had been made to look like a burglary gone wrong, but that didn't tally with the evidence.

For starters, there was no sign of a break-in, so how had the burglar gained entry to the residence? Why had he even chosen this condo as a target? It made absolutely no sense to carry out a burglary in a busy complex at night, when most of the residents would be home. And why had Greg Smart been shot? There were no signs of a struggle inside the house, so why had the burglar put a gun to Greg's head and pulled the trigger? Most burglars didn't even carry guns. No, the more the detectives looked at it, the more the crime scene looked to have been staged. But why? And by whom?

In any domestic homicide, the first suspect is usually the spouse, but in this case, Pamela Smart had a watertight alibi. She'd been 35 miles away, at a school meeting in Hampton. Asked if she knew who might have wanted to hurt her husband, Pam said no. Greg was a wonderful man, loved by everyone who knew him.

Pam and Greg had met at a New Year's Eve party in 1986. They'd found that they enjoyed a mutual love of rock music and had immediately hit it off. A month later they were an item, two years after that they were married. They appeared devoted to one another.

But the marriage was hardly a year old when it was in trouble. Pam felt that Greg was no longer the man she'd fallen in love with. She'd been attracted by his shoulder length hair and fun-loving nature. Now he'd shorn his locks and was making a living, a good living admittedly, as an insurance salesman. Pam had fallen for a rocker. Now, it appeared, she was married to a yuppie.

Worse was to come as they approached their first wedding anniversary. Greg admitted to Pam that he'd been having an affair. It was over now, he said, and he was determined to make their marriage work. A week later, he flew Pam to Florida for an anniversary celebration. On the surface, she forgave him his indiscretion, but whenever they had an argument, she'd bring up his betrayal. Privately, she'd already decided. She wanted out of the marriage.

In the fall of 1989, Pamela was offered a job as media services director with the school board in Hampton, some 35 miles from Derry. Having completed a BA degree at the University of Florida in 1988, she was determined to pursue a career in broadcasting, so this wasn't exactly what she was after. Nonetheless, she believed that it might be a stepping-stone, and so she accepted. Her responsibilities included producing and distributing educational videos for the school district. She was given a full-time secretary and a student intern.

She also volunteered as a facilitator for a school drug awareness program called Project Self-Esteem, where she was soon impressing the kids with her encyclopedic knowledge of rock and heavy metal music. One of those who was definitely impressed was 15-year-old Billy Flynn. The first time he saw Pam, he announced to his friend, Vance "JR" Lattime Jr., "I'm in love."

Pam met Billy Flynn not long after Greg confessed his affair to her. Billy was tall for his age, standing 5-feet-11. He had shoulder-length hair and, like Pam, he loved rock music. He also played the guitar. He was, in other words, everything that Greg no longer was in Pam's eyes. When he began hanging around the SAU building where she worked, she did nothing to discourage him. In fact, she involved him in some of the projects she was working on.

Also around this time, Pam befriended another teenager, Cecelia Pierce, who'd been designated as her student intern. Cecelia wanted to be a journalist and was soon in awe of Pam. Despite the discrepancy in their ages, the two began spending a lot of time together, frequenting malls and restaurants and clubs. Sometimes they hung out at Pam's condo. Billy Flynn usually tagged along.

Pam first hinted to Billy about her feelings for him in February 1990. Three weeks later, they kissed for the first time, while sitting on the bed at Pam's condo. Billy, who was still a virgin at this time, was stunned. Here was this attractive older woman, the object of his boyish fantasies, and she was kissing him, telling him how much she cared for him. Right at that moment, he would have done anything for her. He could not have imagined how soon his juvenile devotion would be put to the test.

Late in March, while Greg was out of town at a conference, Pam invited Billy and Cecelia over to her condo to watch some movies, one of which was 9 ½ Weeks, a steamy thriller starring Kim Basinger and Mickey Rourke. After the movie ended, Pam asked Cecelia to take her Shih Tzu, Halen, for a walk. While Cecelia was away, she took Billy upstairs and they had sex for the first time.

During the weeks that followed, they got together regularly for sex. However, it wasn't long before Pam told Billy that she was going to have to end their relationship. She couldn't let Greg find out about them, she said, otherwise he'd divorce her and she'd lose everything, the condo, the furniture, everything. Worst of all, Greg would take Halen away from her and she couldn't bear to be parted from her little dog. She also hinted that Greg was abusive and that he often beat her.

"If you want to keep seeing me, you'll have to get rid of Greg," she told Billy.

At first, Billy was shocked at the idea, but as Pam kept pressing him, he eventually agreed that he would kill Greg. Twice he put in place advanced plans to carry out the murder but changed his mind at the last moment.

Pam was furious. "If you loved me, you'd do this!" she screamed. Billy said that he did love her. "Then you'd better get rid of Greg, or you're going to lose me," she threatened.

"That's when I started getting serious about it," Billy would later tell the jury at his trial. "Because I thought that if I do something like not go up or anything again, she's going to leave me and that's going be it."

Not long after, Billy started talking to his friends, JR Lattime and Pete Randall, about helping him kill Greg Smart. Pam had told him that May 1 would be his last opportunity. She even threw in a sweetener, offering to pay him and his accomplices out of the insurance money she was going to collect after Greg's death.

Tuesday morning, May 1, played out like any other in the Smart household, with one key difference. Usually, Pam left the house before Greg, but this day she made some excuse to stay behind. The reason was simple. She had to leave a door unlocked so that her young assassins could gain access.

Later that afternoon, Pam spoke to Billy at his school, telling him that the door had been left open as arranged. At around 8:00 p.m., while JR and another teenager, Raymond Fowler, waited in a getaway car, Billy and Pete Randall entered the condo. Their first job was to move Halen down to the basement. Pam had given strict instructions that the dog was not to be harmed or traumatized in any way.

Billy and Pete then ransacked the house, in order to make it look like the murder had happened in the course of a botched robbery. Then the two teenagers waited in the dark for their victim to arrive. Billy had a snub-nosed .38 shoved into his waistband, that JR had taken from his father's gun collection.

At around 8:30, the sweep of a car's headlights briefly illuminated the foyer before being extinguished. The vehicle's engine was cut off. Minutes later came the sound of footfalls of the porch, then a key rattling in the lock. The door swung open, Greg Smart calling out for his dog even before he'd stepped through. Then he was in the foyer and Billy, who'd been hiding behind the door, responded.

He rushed Greg from behind, pushing him to the ground. Then Pete joined the fray and between the two of them they subdued their target. Greg, thinking it was a robbery, told them to take his billfold. Billy raised the gun and held it just two inches from Greg's head. "God forgive me," he said and then pulled the trigger.

Pam Smart's demeanor after the murder surprised investigators. She seemed much too calm, hardly distressed at all. A few days after Greg's death, she asked if she could go back to her home to pick up some things. There, she walked directly through the patch of her dead husband's dried blood on the carpet, barely giving it a second glance. These scarcely seemed like the actions of a grieving widow. It wasn't long before investigators began to suspect that she might have had something to do with Greg's death.

And two weeks later, they had something to hang those suspicions on. An anonymous female tipster called in to say that Pam had persuaded three teenaged boys to kill her husband, and that a girl named Cecelia Pierce knew about it.

On Sunday, June 10, there was another surprise development in the case. JR's father, Vance Lattime Sr., walked into the Seabrook police station and slapped down a snub-nosed .38-caliber revolver on the counter. Lattime said that he'd overheard his son and Pete Randall discussing the murder of Greg Smart and that he believed that this might be the murder weapon.

Things began to fall apart quickly for the conspirators after that. On Monday, June 11, the police brought in Lattime and Randall, as well as Cecelia Pierce. The boys weren't talking, but Pierce eventually broke down and admitted all she knew about the murder, naming Pam Smart and Billy Flynn. The following day, Detectives Pelletier and Charewicz convinced her to help them gather evidence against Pam.

Over the weeks that followed, the police set up two taped phone calls between Cecelia and Pam and also got Cecelia to wear a wire for two meetings between the pair. During the course of those conversations, Pam implicated herself in the murders, stating confidently that, if it came down to her word against that of the boys, the police would believe her.

She was wrong about that. At around 1 p.m. on Wednesday, August 1, officers arrived at Pam Smart's office and took her into custody. The charge was first-degree murder.

Pam Smart went on trial at the Rockingham County Superior Court on March 4, 1991. She readily admitted to having an affair with Billy Flynn but denied that she'd coerced Flynn into killing her husband. According to her version of events, Flynn had become obsessed with her and had killed Greg so that he could have her for himself.

Unfortunately for Pam, the evidence, especially that gathered from her taped conversations with Cecelia Pierce, said otherwise. Found guilty of murder, she was sentenced to life in prison, without the possibility of parole. She remains behind bars to this day, still protesting her innocence.

Of the other defendants, Billy Flynn and Pete Randall each got 40 years in prison, while JR Lattime got 30 years. Lattime's sentence was later reduced and he was released on parole in 2005.

Lizzie Borden Took An Ax

It is one of the most compelling murder mysteries in the history of American crime. According to the famous ditty, Lizzie Borden dispatched her father and stepmother with 81 blows from a hatchet. In truth, the killer was somewhat less frenzied. A total of 29 blows were delivered to 70-year-old Andrew Jackson Borden and his wife, Abby Durfee Gray Borden, 64. Nonetheless, the result was the same. The Bordens were dead and Andrew's younger daughter, Lizzie (33 at the time of the murders), was charged with the crimes.

August 4, 1892, was a stiflingly hot day in Fall River, Massachusetts. At around 11 o'clock that morning, Bridget "Maggie" Sullivan, maid to the Borden family, was resting on the bed in her room. Maggie, like Andrew and Abby Borden, was recovering from a bout of food poisoning and was slightly miffed at being told to clean the windows on such a hot day.

Maggie had only been resting a short while when she was alerted by a cry from downstairs. "Maggie, come down quick! Father's dead. Somebody came in and killed him."

Rushing downstairs, Maggie found Lizzie Borden hovering over the prone form of her father. Andrew Borden lay on a couch, his face bloodied and barely recognizable. He'd been struck so hard that one of his eyeballs was forced from his skull and cleaved in two. Maggie saw no blood on Lizzie, nor any sign of the murder weapon.

Maggie went immediately to summon the police. While Lizzie waited for them to arrive, a neighbor, Adelaide Churchill, came to sit with her. Adelaide went looking for Abby Borden, Lizzie's stepmother, and found her similarly hacked to death. According to later testimony, Abby's body was already cold, while Andrew's was still warm, indicating that Abby had been killed some time before her husband. The pathologist would later estimate that the lapse had been about ninety minutes.

Eventually, the police arrived and carried out a search of the house. They found the scene to be "orderly, with no signs of a scuffle of any kind." This suggested that Andrew had been struck while he slept. In the basement, the police discovered what they believed to be the murder weapon, although the hatchet's handle was missing and there was no blood on it.

Initially, suspicion for the murders fell on a Portuguese laborer, who had called on the Borden home that morning to collect unpaid wages, and been sent away empty-handed. But over the next two

days, the police began to look to Lizzie Borden as their chief
suspect.

A few factors elevated Lizzie to the top of the suspect list. First, a
clerk at S. R. Smith's drug store in Fall River, came forward to tell
police that Lizzie had tried to buy prussic acid, a deadly poison,
just a few days prior to the murders. Then, there were rumors of
Lizzie's strained relationship with her stepmother. And Lizzie's
alibi for the time of the murders hardly allayed suspicion. She said
she'd been in a barn looking for fishing sinkers. But the loft where
she claimed to have been looking was thick with dust that had not
been recently disturbed.

Lastly, there was the matter of opportunity. According to Maggie
Sullivan, Lizzie and her parents had been the only people in the
house. Lizzie's older sister, Emma, had been 15 miles away,
visiting relatives in Fairhaven, Massachusetts. A houseguest, John
Morse, was away running errands.

The inquest into the Borden murders was held at the Fall River
courthouse on August 9. Lizzie, exhausted by the police
investigation and the media furor the case was kicking up, had
been prescribed morphine to calm her nerves. She spent four
hours on the witness stand, delivering testimony that was garbled
and contradictory. Two days later, she found herself under arrest,
charged with two counts of murder.

Lizzie was sent to the jailhouse at Taunton, eight miles north of
Fall River. On August 22, she was back in Fall River for a
preliminary hearing. She entered a plea of "Not Guilty" but the

presiding judge found that there was enough evidence to convene a grand jury. When that body met in November, they seemed disinclined to issue an indictment. What swayed them was the evidence of Alice Russell, a family friend who had stayed at the Borden residence in the days following the murders.

Russell testified that she had seen Lizzie Borden burning a blue frock in the kitchen stove. When questioned about this unusual action, Lizzie said that the dress was damaged due to her getting paint on it. It had earlier been reported (by Maggie Sullivan) that Lizzie had been wearing just such a dress on the day of the murders.

Lizzie Borden's trial began on June 5, 1893, in the New Bedford Courthouse, a panel of three judges presiding. The Borden sisters had assembled a powerful defense team, led by former Massachusetts' governor, George Robinson. The state was represented by District Attorney Knowlton, assisted by William H. Moody, a future Supreme Court judge.

The prosecution case was built around motive and opportunity. Who but Lizzie had the opportunity to kill her parents, Moody postulated? Who else might want them dead? Yet he was unable to provide any substantiating evidence to support his claims, something that George Robinson used to his full advantage. If Lizzie had so brutally slain her parents, then surely she'd have been covered in blood? And yet the police found none, not even a speck on the alleged murder weapon.

In the end, there was never going to be enough evidence to obtain a guilty verdict, and so it proved. On June 20, 1893, the twelve-man jury deliberated for just an hour-and-a-half before returning a verdict of "Not Guilty." On hearing the pronouncement, Lizzie let out a cry, then slumped back in her seat with her hands covering her face, as her sister and other well-wishers rushed forward to congratulate her.

Lizzie and Emma Borden were the sole beneficiaries of their father's considerable estate. After the trial, the sisters remained in Fall River where they bought an impressive mansion on "The Hill," the city's most exclusive area. Most of the citizens of Fall River continued to believe that Lizzie Borden had killed her parents and she and Emma were generally ostracized. Not that it appeared to worry Lizzie much. She became a patron of the arts and was known to associate with actors and other "theatrical types." In later years, she and Emma had a falling out and Emma moved out of their shared home in 1923. Lizzie remained there until her death in 1927, aged 67. She was buried beside her parents in Fall River's Oak Grove Cemetery.

But the question remains: If Lizzie Borden did not murder her parents, then who did? A number of suspects have been put forward over the years, including Emma Borden, Maggie Sullivan, the mysterious Portuguese laborer, and an alleged illegitimate son of Andrew Borden's who was angered after an attempt to extort money from his father failed. The truth is that none of these so-called suspects makes as compelling a murderer as Lizzie Borden.

Only she had the opportunity. She was alone in the house with the victims and given that the murders occurred ninety minutes apart,

an outside killer would have had to hide in the house for that time
before carrying out the second murder. An unlikely scenario.

There was also no evidence of forced entry. No strangers were
seen entering or leaving the Borden residence on the morning of
the murders, and no valuables were missing from the house.
Despite Abby Borden putting up a valiant fight for her life, Lizzie,
who was just downstairs, reported hearing no sounds of a
struggle. Maggie Sullivan heard something, though, a laugh, which
she thought was Lizzie, coming from upstairs. Lizzie claimed she
was never there.

Then there were Lizzie's convoluted attempts at an alibi. Her claim
that she'd been in the loft was proven to be untrue. She also
claimed that a messenger had delivered a note to her stepmother
on the day of the murders, summoning her to visit a sick friend.
(This was given as a reason why she didn't call out to her
stepmother on discovering her father's body). No trace of the note
or messenger was ever found.

There was also an effort on her part to raise suspicion before the
event. On the night before the murders, Lizzie visited her
neighbor, Alice Russell, and told her that she feared one of her
father's enemies might try to kill him.

It was, of course, the same neighbor who spotted Lizzie destroying
the blue dress, just days after the murder, the dress she'd been
wearing on that fateful day.

As far as motive goes, it was well known that Lizzie had a strained relationship with her stepmother. She was also reportedly angry with her father over a property he refused to sign over to her. The last straw appears to have been Andrew Borden's killing of Lizzie's pigeons, who he claimed attracted thieves to his property.

On August 3, the day before the murders, Lizzie called on Smith's drug store in Fall River and attempted to buy prussic acid. The pharmacist refused to sell her the deadly poison, and so Lizzie Borden took an ax.

Death On A Sunday

Ian Huntley

On the afternoon of Sunday, August 4, 2002, best friends Holly Wells and Jessica Chapman left a family barbecue to walk to a nearby sports center, to buy candy. The ten-year- olds were both wearing the colors of their favorite soccer team, Manchester United, the name of their favorite player, David Beckham, adorning the back. An hour passed and with the day heading towards dark and the girls still not returned, their parents began to worry. Then, after Jessica's father tried to call her cell phone and got no response, a search was launched. No trace of the girls was found along the route they would have walked, no one at the sports club remembered having seen them. Their frantic parents then drove to the nearest police station and reported them missing.

A search team, involving police and hundreds of volunteers, was quickly assembled and began scouring the area. Yet as a new day dawned, there was no trace of them and the police began to fear the worst. Holly and Jessica had certainly not become lost in an area they knew well. The only other possibilities were that they'd been kidnapped or killed.

Days turned to weeks and despite the searches, despite the missing persons posters, despite the public appeals from the girls' parents, no trace of them was found. Even a televised appeal for their safe return by Manchester United soccer star, David Beckham, failed to deliver any result. Hopes for their safety began to dwindle; the focus began to shift from finding them alive, to catching whoever had taken them.

By now, of course, the police had assembled reams of witness statements regarding the disappearance. One of those was from Ian Huntley, a 29-year-old caretaker, employed by the nearby Soham Village College. Huntley had volunteered to assist in the search and had been interviewed on TV regarding his participation in the case. His witness statement informed investigators that the girls had passed by his house on the day they went missing. He knew them vaguely, he said, because his girlfriend, Maxine Carr, was a teaching assistant at their school.

After reading Huntley's statement, the police realized that he must have been one of the last people to see Holly and Jessica alive. That made him a person of interest in the case and although he was not suspected of involvement, the police asked if they could search his home. Huntley readily agreed. The search turned up nothing incriminating.

However, Huntley had roused the suspicions of senior detectives. They knew from experience that a certain class of killer often seeks to insert himself into the investigation and Huntley's behavior seemed to fit this pattern. He asked too many questions, appeared too emotionally involved with girls he claimed he hardly knew. He also came across as smug, as though he knew a secret he wasn't telling. A second search was authorized, this time including Huntley's work premises. It was there that the police hit paydirt.

At Soham Village College, an officer located a garbage bin containing burned remnants of Holly and Jessica's Manchester United shirts, as well as the charred remains of their shoes. Huntley was arrested on suspicion of murder soon after. Maxine Carr was arrested as an accessory.

But although the police now had a murder suspect in custody they had as yet been unable to locate the alleged murder victims. That issue was to be tragically resolved on August 17, 2002, 13 days since Holly and Jessica had disappeared. A game warden was patrolling the woods near the RAF air base at Lakenheath, when he came across a six-foot ditch containing what appeared to be charred human remains. The bodies were later removed to the morgue where an autopsy would list the probable cause of death as asphyxiation.

Ian Huntley, meanwhile, had rapidly become a national hate figure, especially after the media began showing footage of him participating in the search for the missing girls and expressing concern for their wellbeing. The questions a grieving nation wanted answered were: Who on earth was this monster, and what might have possessed him to so callously end the lives of two innocent young girls?

Ian Huntley was born in Grimsby on January 31, 1974, the first son of Kevin Huntley and his wife Linda. As a child, he was subjected to severe bullying, the problem escalating to the point where his parents had to move him to a new school. There, he eventually graduated with a B average although he decided to find employment rather than attend college.

Over the next 10 years, Huntley worked at various unskilled jobs. During this period he began to attract the attention of the police. No fewer than ten rape allegations were leveled at him and he was also arrested for burglary, indecent assault, and sex with a minor. In 1995, he married Claire Evans, but the couple soon separated and eventually divorced in 1999. A year later, Claire married Huntley's younger brother, Wayne.

In February 1999, Huntley met Maxine Carr at a nightclub in Grimsby. They soon moved in together, sharing an apartment in Barton-upon-Humber, while Carr worked at a fish processing plant and Huntley worked as a barman. On his days off he'd travel to Littleport, where his father had a job as a caretaker at the village school. Huntley enjoyed helping his father so much that he decided to apply for similar work himself. It was thus that he came to be employed by Soham Village College, beginning in November 2001. Less than a year later he'd stand accused of the murders of Holly Wells and Jessica Chapman.

The evidence against Huntley was growing daily. Fibers found in his house were matched to the clothes Holly and Jessica were wearing. Hairs and fibers found on the remnants of the soccer jerseys were matched to Huntley and to his home and car. The police were also able to track the last signal from Jessica's cell phone to the location of Huntley's home. In addition, it was learned that Huntley often spent time plane spotting near the woods where the girls' bodies were found.

Cell phone records were used to clear Maxine Carr from direct involvement in the murders. However, they landed her firmly in the mix as an accessory. Carr had claimed that she'd been in the house with Huntley on the day the girls disappeared. Records showed that she was in Grimsby, visiting her mother, at the time of the girls' abduction and murders.

Yet despite the mountain of evidence against him, Ian Huntley continued to protest his innocence. It would be up to the Crown to prove otherwise.

The trial of Huntley and Carr began at London's famous Old Bailey Courthouse on November 3, 2003. The prosecution was led by Richard Latham QC. Over the opening weeks of the trial, he presented a compelling case against Huntley. In addition to the forensic evidence mentioned earlier, there were fingerprints and eyewitness testimony of how Huntley had tried to cover his tracks, ripping out carpets from his car, burning a rug and replacing the tires on his vehicle, even though they were relatively new. Despite these measures, the police had found traces of chalk, concrete, and soil that were matched to the dumpsite.

Huntley listened dispassionately to this evidence for three weeks. Inside, though, he must have known that his denials had been exposed as a lie. Eventually, he cracked and accepted responsibility for the girls' deaths. He now claimed they were accidental

Huntley was not present in court on the day that his defense counsel read out his, frankly ridiculous, statement. He'd cried off ill.

According to Huntley's revised testimony, Holly and Jessica had called at his home on August 4, 2002, looking for Maxine Carr. While they were there, Holly had suffered a nosebleed and Huntley had led her to the bathroom to get some tissues to treat it. While he was doing so, he'd accidently knocked her backward and she'd fallen into the bathtub, which was half full with water.

On seeing her friend fall, Jessica had started screaming. Huntley had tried to keep her quiet by putting his hand over her mouth. In the process, he'd accidently suffocated her. He'd then looked down at Holly in the bathtub and realized that she had drowned. Panicked, Huntley had then put the girls' bodies into his car and driven them to Lakenheath. There he'd cut off their clothes, poured gasoline over their corpses and set them alight.

Hampered by the ridiculous story their client was trying to sell the court, the defense began making its case on December 1, 2003. Only two witnesses were called, Huntley and Carr. Both were torn to shreds on cross-examination by Latham.

Eventually, on December 12, the case went to the jury. They returned five days later with their decision. Huntley and Carr were both found guilty. He was sentenced to life in prison, she to three-and-a-half years.

Huntley's life in prison has been difficult. In September 2005 he suffered scalding after a fellow inmate threw boiling water in his face. A year later, he was found unconscious in his cell after swallowing a handful of anti-depressants in an apparent suicide attempt. In March 2010, he was rushed to hospital after being slashed across the throat by another prisoner. The wounds were ruled to be superficial, but that didn't stop Huntley demanding £20,000 compensation for his injuries. Holly and Jessica's parents had received £11,000 in the wake of their daughters' deaths.

The Fugitive

If there were two things that defined John List, they were his religious beliefs and his profession. The devout Christian was a regular attendee at the local Lutheran church, where he sometimes taught Sunday school. He worked as an accountant, a vocation perfectly suited to his meticulous and somewhat frugal nature.

Given that frugality, it was perhaps surprising that in 1965, he splashed out on a home that he could scarcely afford. The three-story, 18-room Victorian mansion was in Westfield, New Jersey. It had once been home to the millionaire John S.A. Wittke. Now it was home to the List family, John, his wife, Helen, children, Patricia Marie, 16, John Fredrick, 15, and Fredrick Michael, 13, and his 85-year-old mother, Alma.

Things went swimmingly for the next five years. John was the vice president of a bank, and earning good money. His children were growing up in what he considered a good Christian town, and attending weekly services at the Redeemer Lutheran church. He hadn't made many friends in Westfield, but that was how he preferred it. He didn't want his family exposed to corrupting outside influences.

But as the decade wound to a close, things began to go awry for John List. First, he lost his job at the bank. No problem, he soon got another. But that one was short-lived and so was the next. Embarrassed by his failure to hold down a job, List decided not to tell his family that he was unemployed. He continued his normal routine, leaving for the office each day, returning each evening. He'd spend the day at the railway station, reading, napping and silently raging at his bad fortune. Meanwhile, the bills kept piling up and List was becoming increasingly desperate. He felt that he'd let his family down. He saw no way out of the financial morass he'd fallen into.

Then came the day when he received a foreclosure notice on his home and List made a horrific decision. He couldn't allow his family to be humiliated and thrown out on the street. He decided to spare them that indignity by killing them.

The murder of his family, like everything else in John List's life, was meticulously planned. The date he chose was November 9, 1971. That morning he waited until his three children had left for school, then went out to his car and loaded his two pistols, a .22 and a 9mm German-made Steyr. He then walked back to the house and entered the kitchen, where his wife, Helen, sat drinking a cup of coffee. Walking up behind her, he lifted the pistol and drilled a single bullet into her brain. Helen was dead before she knew what

was happening. List lowered her to the tiled floor and then headed
for the staircase.

List's mother, Alma, was sitting down to breakfast in the suite of
rooms she occupied on the upper floor. As List entered, she asked
him about the noise she'd heard from downstairs. He didn't reply.
Instead, he walked up behind her, stooped to give her a kiss on the
cheek and then placed the Steyr against the side of her head and
pulled the trigger. Alma List died instantly. Her son then left her
room, closing the door behind him.

It was now barely 9:30 and John List had already committed two
murders. Returning to the kitchen, he mopped up the blood from
the tile. Then he went upstairs and tried, less successfully, to clean
the blood from his mother's carpeted bedroom floor. That task
completed, he went to the basement and carried up the sleeping
bags that the family used for camping. Flipping Helen's body onto
the bag he dragged her through the house and into the huge,
unfurnished ballroom to the rear.

List now had time to fill before his children returned from school,
and he wasn't a wasteful man. First, he collected up old photo
family albums and destroyed every photograph in which he
appeared. Next, he wrote letters to four relatives, explaining his
motives for the murders. With time still to spare, he phoned
Barbara Bader, a local parent who usually gave his sons a ride to
school. He told her that the family was going to be leaving for
North Carolina the following morning, to visit his wife's mother,
who he claimed was ill. He promised to let her know when they
returned.

After hanging up with Barbara Bader, List made a few similar calls, offering the same story to people who might notice the unexplained disappearance of his family. As the List clan was reclusive, there weren't many. He did, however, have to cancel the newspaper delivery, milk delivery, and mail delivery. He also had to make excuses at his children's schools. Those tasks completed, List prepared lunch, eating it at the same table where he'd killed his wife just hours before.

As he ate, List was mulling over a problem. He was worried that two of his children, Patricia and John, might arrive home from school at the same time and wasn't sure how he'd handle it if they did. Then the phone rang and that problem was solved for him. It was Patricia, saying that she felt unwell and asking if he'd collect her from school early. List happily did so. Patricia had barely entered the house when he shot her in the head with his .22 caliber pistol.

Patricia was rolled onto one of the sleeping bags and dragged into the ballroom where she was placed beside her mother. Then, after mopping up her blood from the foyer, List left again, this time, to pick up Fredrick, his youngest son, from his after school job. As List pulled up in front of the house with Fred in the passenger seat, he saw his other son, John, turn the corner onto their road. He quickly hustled Fredrick inside, shooting him as he stepped through the door. Then he waited on John's arrival.

John was the only family member to suffer multiple gunshot wounds. List would later offer two explanations for that. First, he said that he'd done so to ensure that John, his favorite, was dead and wasn't suffering. On another occasion, he admitted that the extreme emotion of the day got to him and he lost control.

John List had now butchered his entire family. But the task he'd set himself was far from completed. First, he dragged Fredrick and John to join their mother and sister in what had now become a makeshift mausoleum. Then he mopped up the blood of his two sons before retiring to his study where he composed a five-page letter to his pastor, Eugene Rehwinkel. This document offers the most detailed confession that John List ever gave. In it, he bemoans his precarious financial position, which drove him to such extreme measures. However, he also offered another motive for the murders. He claimed that his family had begun to stray from the path of righteousness and that he'd killed them in order to save their immortal souls. The letter ended with a postscript. "P.S. Mother is in the hallway in the attic-third floor. She was too heavy to move."

By the time the letter was composed to List's satisfaction, it was 6 p.m. and already dark. Having built up an appetite through the afternoon's exertions, he sat down to a meal, then did the dishes before making yet another phone call. This one was to Barbara Sheridan, with whom Patricia took acting classes at the Westfield Recreation Commission. He gave her the same story about the family having to travel to North Carolina. Barbara thanked him for the call and said she'd inform the workshop director, Edwin Illiano.

Having completed his last scheduled task, John List climbed the stairs to the bedroom he'd shared with his murdered wife. While she and their three children lay dead on the cold floor of the ballroom, he tucked himself into a warm bed and was soon fast asleep.

The following morning, List rose early and went about his ablutions. That completed, he adjusted the thermostat down to its lowest setting, turned on a recorder with classical music set to continue playing in a loop, and switched on every light in the house. Then he locked his front door, got into his 1963 Chevrolet Impala, and drove away from Westfield forever.

Over the next month, neighbors commented often about the lights being constantly on in the List house. Yet nobody thought of knocking on the door to check on the family. Perhaps they'd heard that the Lists were out of town and assumed that the lights had been left on to deter burglars. Whatever the case, it wasn't until December 7, that somebody finally decided to investigate.

Edwin Illiano, the director of the drama workshop that Patricia List was enrolled in, started to become concerned about the family's prolonged absence. He recalled a conversation he'd had with Patricia when she'd confided her fears that her father might be planning to hurt her and her family. Over dinner one night, John List had apparently asked each member of his family what they wanted done with their remains after they were dead.

Illiano eventually decided to call on the List home, taking his associate, Barbara Sheridan, with him. On arriving at the house, the pair first tried knocking on the door. Getting no reply they began circling the property, peering into windows.   While they were doing so, one of the Lists' neighbors spotted them and called the police.

Patrolmen George Zhelesnik and Charles Haller were the first on the scene. Listening earnestly as Illiano expressed his concerns, the officers decided to break in. The smell that greeted them when they stepped into the foyer told them that Illiano's suspicions had been right.

John List, by now, had a 29 day lead on the police. After leaving Westfield, he'd driven his car to John F. Kennedy International Airport in New York. Abandoning the vehicle there to confuse his pursuers, he'd taken a bus into the city and from there had boarded a Greyhound, heading west. He'd traveled to Denver, where he'd assumed the name Robert P. Clark and found work as a short order cook. He would remain at large for 18 years, during which time he'd return to his chosen profession as an accountant, marry a widow named Delores, and eventually settle in Richmond, Virginia. He must have thought that he'd gotten away with murder.

However, List had underestimated the determination of the Union County Prosecutor's Office to bring him to justice. Over the nearly two decades that List was a fugitive, that office followed up countless leads, investigated numerous sightings, chased down hundreds of clues, no matter how slim.

In 1989, the now (very) cold case landed on the desk of Captain Frank Marranca. By now, law enforcement officials across the country had a new weapon in the fight against crime, the television show, America's Most Wanted. Marranca wanted a slot on the show for the List case. The producers said no. Marranca persisted until they eventually gave in.

On Sunday evening, May 21, 1989, the show flighted an eight-minute segment on John List, including a life-like bust, molded by forensic sculptor Frank Bender. The sculpture was designed to show what List might look like now, eighteen years since he'd gone on the run. It would prove to be amazingly accurate.

List was, in fact, watching the show when it aired, his new wife sitting beside him. She made no comment about the remarkable likeness, but one of List's old neighbors back in Denver thought that it looked a lot like Robert P. Clark, who had since moved to Richmond, Virginia. The man phoned in his suspicions to the police. List was arrested 11 days later.

John List was extradited to New Jersey, where on April 12, 1990, he was convicted of five counts of first-degree murder. On May 1, he was sentenced to five terms of life in prison.

List would spend almost as long behind bars as he had on the run, dying of pneumonia on March 21, 2008, at the age of 82.

There is an interesting footnote to the John List story. The List home in Westfield burned to the ground under mysterious circumstances shortly after the murders. While demolition work was in progress it was discovered that the glass ceiling in the ballroom, where List had left his murdered family, was a signed Tiffany & Co. original. That alone would have fetched enough to clear all of John List's debts, and left him with money to spare.

Unhinged

In the aftermath of the tragedy, many would ask the question, why? Why did no one try to help this obviously disturbed woman? Why was she not red-flagged? Why was she not institutionalized? Why was such a deranged individual allowed to legally purchase not one, but three, firearms? Why?

The answers, if there are any, are elusive. Some relate to individual freedoms, others to misguided parental love, still others to societal indifference. The fact is that Laurie Wasserman Dann should have been in an institution long before that fateful day in May 1988, when she roamed the streets of Winnetka, Illinois, with her poisoned snacks, gasoline canister, and .32 Smith and Wesson revolver.

Laurie Wasserman was born on October 18, 1957, in Chicago, Illinois. Her father, Norman, was a successful accountant, and Laurie grew up in the affluent Chicago suburb of Glencoe. She wanted for nothing during her formative years, but she was an awkward, unattractive girl. That is, until her parents gave her the gift of plastic surgery. Under the point of the surgeon's knife, the ugly duckling was transformed into a beautiful, dark-haired girl, who was soon attracting suitors.

After graduating from New Trier East High School, Laurie was accepted at the University of Arizona and spent four years at study there, although she never graduated. That had never been the intention anyway. Laurie was attending college with the sole purpose of snaring a wealthy husband. She thought that she'd succeeded when she became engaged to a premed student. She was devastated when he ended the relationship. With very little interest in continuing her education in Arizona, she returned to her parents' home in 1980.

Still hurting from her failed relationship, Laurie had no particular plans for her future. She attended various adult education classes, but rarely finished a course. She also worked at a number of low-paying jobs, one of those as a waitress at the Green Acres Country Club in Northbrook. It was there that she met Russell Dann, a handsome young man from a wealthy Highland Park family.

Dann was immediately entranced by the pretty, dark-haired woman, and she was by no means averse to his attentions. The couple began dating, and married in September 1982, moving into a luxurious $230,000 Highland Park home.

However, wedded bliss was short-lived. Just days into the marriage, Russell began to realize that his new wife was no homemaker. He'd return from work to find the house a mess of unmade beds and dirty dishes piled up in the sink, while Laurie lay sprawled on the sofa watching TV. And on the occasions that she did make an attempt at housework, the results were unpredictable. One time she did the laundry, folded up the still wet clothing and packed it away in various closets. She also liked to keep things in odd places. Her makeup was stored in the microwave, for example, and she didn't use a purse to hold her cash. She simply scattered the notes and coins on the back seat of her car. And then there were her little rituals, like obsessive hand washing, and tapping her foot against the floor of her car every time she stopped at a traffic light.

Eventually, those behaviors would take their toll on the marriage and the couple separated in October 1985. Divorce proceedings were acrimonious, with Laurie accusing Russell of spousal abuse. During this time, Russell and his family began to be harassed by hang up phone calls.

In April 1986, Laurie accused her husband of breaking in and vandalizing her parents' home. Shortly after, she obtained a gun license and purchased a .357 Magnum. Then, in September 1986, Russell Dann was attacked in his house and stabbed with an ice pick while he slept. He pointed the finger at Laurie, but she denied the accusation and agreed to a polygraph, which she passed with flying colors. No charges were brought. Evidence would later emerge that Laurie had purchased an ice pick, similar to the one used to stab Russell, just days before the attack.

In May 1987, the Danns' marriage was officially dissolved, with Laurie banking a $125,000 settlement. But if Russell Dann thought that he'd seen the last of his ex-wife, he was sorely mistaken. She continued to make harassing calls to him and his family and to lay wild charges against him with the police. She claimed that he'd raped her with a steak knife and that he'd planted a bomb in her parents home. No charges were officially laid against Russell, but Laurie's parents firmly believed her claims and continued to support her.

And Russell Dann wasn't the only target of Laurie's harassment. Her former boyfriend in Arizona reported to the police that she'd been making death threats against his family and claiming to be pregnant with his child, even though he'd last seen her over five years ago. She'd also sent an anonymous letter to the hospital where he worked, claiming to be a patient who had been raped by him. The harassment would continue until Norman Wasserman received a lawyer's letter, asking him to rein in his daughter.

In January 1987, Laurie posted a notice at the Glencoe public library and at a local grocery store, offering her services as a babysitter. One mother, obviously unaware of her history, offered her a job and found her to be pleasant, soft-spoken, and excellent with children. She was soon recommending Laurie to her friends.

But, as with everything in Laurie Dann's life, the veneer of sanity soon wore thin. Parents began to notice misarranged objects in their homes after Laurie had been there, slashes to rugs and sofas, small objects missing. One couple went as far as filing a police complaint, but there was no hard evidence and no charges were brought. Nonetheless, Laurie's once thriving babysitting business soon ground to a halt.

In the summer of 1987, Laurie delighted her parents by announcing that she was returning to college to complete her degree. Norman Wasserman, as ever attentive to his daughter's needs, rented her a university apartment in Evanston, Illinois. It wasn't long before students were complaining about raw meat being left to rot under cushions in common rooms, and about garbage pushed into their mailboxes. The culprit was soon identified. Norman Dann was politely asked to remove his daughter from the university.

And he was soon dealing with a new crisis of his daughter's making. Duping a new set of mothers into hiring her as a babysitter, she began causing damage to their property and stealing hundreds of dollars worth of food. Norman as always, covered her tracks, paying restitution and pleading with her victims not to file charges. Nobody did.

It seems strange that Norman Wasserman, so attentive to his daughter's needs, did not comprehend what in retrospect seems obvious. Laurie Dann needed psychiatric care. She needed to be institutionalized. Instead, she was allowed to strike out on her own again in January of 1988. This time, she moved to Madison and enrolled at the University of Wisconsin.

All too soon, Laurie's strange behavior began to attract attention. In addition to her old habit of leaving raw meat to rot wherever she went, she developed a compulsion for riding the elevator at all times of the day and night. She also took to wearing rubber gloves and shying away from metal surfaces. She was seen on occasion wandering the halls naked, but most of the time barricaded herself in her dorm room, which she turned into a health hazard, with rotting food and garbage everywhere.

In the fall of 1987, Dann again reported her ex-husband to the police. She claimed that he'd written threatening letters and that he'd sexually assaulted her in a parking lot. When her story wasn't believed, she became angry. A few weeks later, she purchased a second revolver, a .32 caliber Smith and Wesson.

In March 1988, Dann started making preparations for the attacks she'd eventually carry out. She began stealing library books on poisons and pilfering arsenic from the chemistry lab. She also started a concerted shoplifting operation, accumulating clothes and wigs that she intended using to disguise herself. During this time she also escalated her campaign of threatening phone calls, targeting the Dann family, her ex-boyfriend, and her former babysitting clients. Also in March, she was arrested for shoplifting but avoided jail time.

She was suspected of arson in April, after a fire started in one of the dorm rooms at the university. No charges were brought. In the meantime, an FBI investigation had been launched into the death threats made against her Arizona boyfriend. During the course of that inquiry, it was determined that Dann legally owned three firearms. When the police arrived at the Wasserman residence to request the voluntary surrender of the weapons, Norman Wasserman refused. He insisted that his daughter needed the guns for protection against her ex-husband.

By now, Laurie Dann's descent into madness had passed the tipping point. On May 14, a student at the university returned to find that his clothing and books had been shredded. Laurie was implicated and a search was launched for her. She was found later that night, sleeping naked in a pile of garbage, covered only by a plastic bag. Before any disciplinary action could be launched, she disappeared from the campus and returned to Glencoe. The end game was in play. Laurie Dann was preparing for a massacre.

On the evening of May 19, 1988, Dann stayed up late, making rice crispy snacks laced with arsenic and injecting poison into pre-packaged fruit juice. The following morning, she mailed several packages of the poisoned snacks to former acquaintances, babysitting clients, and to her psychiatrist. She then personally delivered her toxic treats to a number of homes in Glencoe as well as to various fraternity houses at Northwestern University in Evanston.

Then, she went to pick up the sons of one of her babysitting clients for a prearranged day out. Leaving the residence, she drove to Ravinia Elementary School, where her former sister-in-law's children were pupils. There she started a fire, before fleeing. Next, she drove to the daycare center that her ex-sister-in-law's daughter attended. Her plan was to start another fire, but a staff member saw her carrying a gasoline can and told her to leave.

A short while later, Dann returned the boys to their home. She gave them each a glass of milk but they refused to drink it, saying it tasted funny (the milk was later positively tested for arsenic). She then brought the boys down to the basement where their mother was doing laundry. She mumbled some excuse as to why she'd had to cancel the day out and then left. Moments later, the children's mother smelled smoke. She went to investigate and saw that the basement stairs were ablaze. She and her sons escaped by breaking a small window and crawling to safety.

Dann had meanwhile entered the nearby Hubbard Woods Elementary School, carrying a gun in each hand, like a movie assassin. Seeing a boy exiting a washroom, she shot at him, hitting him in the stomach. Next, she entered a second-grade classroom and began firing wildly. Eight-year-old Nicholas Corwin was killed instantly. Five others were critically injured.

Thankfully, Dann did not venture any further into the school. She fled in her car, traveling just a few blocks before colliding with a tree. Then she reloaded her weapons, left the vehicle, and entered the home of the Andrews family. She claimed that she had shot a man who had raped her and that the police were now hunting her. She needed a place to hide out.

Over the next six hours, Dann held the family hostage. During that time, she made a call to her mother, who begged her to turn herself in. Laurie said she'd think about it.

Eventually, Phillip Andrews, 20, convinced her to let the rest of his family go, while he remained as a hostage. Laurie agreed, but as soon as the family was safe, Phillip tried to wrestle the gun away. A shot was fired, hitting him in the chest. He staggered out of the house and collapsed on the front lawn.

With the police closing in on the house, Laurie Dann then climbed the stairs to an upstairs bedroom, put her revolver in her mouth, and blew her own brains out.

Laurie Dann's rampage had left an eight-year-old boy dead, and seven people seriously injured. Several others had to be treated for arsenic poisoning, smoke inhalation, and other injuries. Still, others had to receive trauma counseling.

In the wake of the tragedy, it was revealed that Dann had been seeing psychiatrists for obsessive-compulsive disorders for many years. She was also thought to be suffering from "erotomania," a tendency towards forming pathological attachments to men she believed were in love with her. She'd been taking both lithium and anafranil. Both drugs can cause violence in patients.

For more True Crime books by Robert Keller please visit

http://bit.ly/kellerbooks

Printed in Great Britain
by Amazon